Innovating Faculty Development

Entering the Age of Innovation

*By Charlie Sweet, Hal Blythe
& Russell Carpenter*

NEW FORUMS

NEW FORUMS PRESS INC.

Published in the United States of America
by New Forums Press, Inc.1018 S. Lewis St.
Stillwater, OK 74074
www.newforums.com

Copyright © 2016 by New Forums Press, Inc.

All rights reserved. No part of this publication may be reproduced or transmitted in any form or by any means, electronic or mechanical, including photocopy, or any information storage or retrieval system, without permission in writing from the publisher.

Library of Congress Cataloging-in-Publication Data Pending

This book may be ordered in bulk quantities at discount from New Forums Press, Inc., P.O. Box 876, Stillwater, OK 74076 [Federal I.D. No. 73 1123239]. Printed in the United States of America.

ISBN 10: 1-58107-297-X
ISBN 13: 978-1-58107-297-6

Contents

INTRODUCTION vii
FOUNDATIONAL THEORY 1
A. The Importance of Creative Thinking to Academia's Future 3
    1. Why Successful Faculty Development Requires Innovation 4
    2. How to Weave Creative Thinking into the Institutional Fabric 5
    3. Using Creative Thinking to Innovate Faculty Development 7
    4. Tuesday Mornings 9
B. Applying Creative Thinking to Faculty Development 11
    1. How Design Thinking Helps Innovate Faculty Development, Part I 12
    2. How Design Thinking Helps Innovate Faculty Development, Part II 14
    3. The Faculty Developer's Most Important Question 16
    4. Applying Pedagogy as the Fifth Creative Thinking Perspective 17
    5. Creating Unified Higher Ed Faculty Development Programming 19
    6. Resources on Unifying Faculty Development Programming 20
    7. 3 Principles for Innovating the Faculty Development Experience 22
    8. The Future of Faculty Development: A Techtonic Shift 24
    9. Is There Really a Teaching Revival Happening Now? 26

**ESTABLISHING A CENTER OF TEACHING
AND LEARNING (CTL)** 29
    1. Why Centers of Teaching and Learning Have Advisory Boards 31
    2. What Services Should a Center of Teaching and Learning Offer 33
    3. Types and Characteristics of Successful Faculty Programming 37
    4. 14 Guidelines for Successful Higher Ed Faculty Workshops 40
    5. To Belong or Not Belong to POD in Higher Education? 43
    6. Is Your Center of Teaching and Learning a Hammer or Nail? 45
    7. The X-Factor: One Result of Success 47

CREATING A FACULTY DEVELOPMENT PROGRAM ... 51

A. Instituting Faculty Innovators and The Faculty Innovation Network ... 53

1. Faculty Innovators: The Key to the Future of Faculty Development ... 54
2. Behind the Scenes with Wizards Behind the Faculty Innovators ... 56
3. How to Select Faculty Innovators ... 58
4. An Inside Look at a Faculty Innovator Progress, Part I ... 61
5. An Inside Look at a Faculty Innovator Progress, Part II ... 62
6. Using Technology to Build the Faculty Innovation Network ... 64
7. Funding the Faculty Innovator Program ... 67

B. Determining Services For Individuals ... 71

1. Faculty Development: Consultation and Classroom Observation ... 72
2. The Heisenberg Effect: A Flaw in Classroom Observation ... 74

C. Determining Services For Groups: New Faculty, Part-time, First-Year Course Instructors, TAs ... 77

1. How to Improve Faculty Attendance at Higher Ed Professional Development Events ... 78
2. Innovating Faculty Development Lessons from Pedagogy Day ... 80
3. How to Communicate Best Practices in Higher Ed Pedagogy ... 82
4. Another Approach to Pedagogy Day ... 84

D. Focused Faculty Groups: PLCs, Breakfast & a Books, and Creative Communities ... 87

1. Focused Faculty Groups: Breakfast and a Book ... 88
2. The Best Center of Teaching and Learning Service for Professional Development ... 90
3. How to Assess Professional Learning Communities ... 93
4. The Great Professional Learning Community Experiment ... 95
5. The Higher Education Professional Learning Community Oversight ... 97
6. A Third Type of Community ... 99

E. Implementing Innovative Pedagogical Strategies 103
1. A Reaction to Worthen's 'Lecture Me, Really' 104
2. Flipping the Classroom, New Book in It Works for Me Series 106
3. Making it C.R.I.S.P. 108
4. Applying C.R.I.S.P. to Change Higher Education Campus Culture 111
5. The Four Rs of Deep Learning 113
6. The Importance of Physical Space for Faculty Performance 114
7. 7 Tips for Making the Most of Higher Ed Instructional Videos 117

F. Promoting Scholarship 121
1. Kentucky Pedagogicon: How We Did It 122
2. Making of Pedagogicon Conference Via Nifty-Nine Strategies 124
3. Scholarship Lite 125
4. Under Construction: Developing a Style Sheet for the *Journal of Faculty Development* 128
5. Collaboration and the Scholar 130

ASSESSMENT 133
1. Going to WAR: Using a Weekly Activities Report for Assessment, Part I ... 134
2. Going to WAR: Using a Weekly Activities Report for Assessment, Part II .. 135
3. An Innovative Plan for Assessing Faculty Development 137

AFTERWORD 141

ABOUT THE AUTHORS 143

Note from the Publisher

The articles provided in this collection are derived from blog posts published on the New Forums Press Web site, www.newforums.com, over a period of two years as the authors put into writing their ideas about innovating faculty development. They have been edited and organized in this volume so as to provide the reader with an orderly and coherent presentation of the concepts that evolved. While for the most part the same material offered here is available free online, this book provides immediate access to the concepts the authors present as well as some new content.

Many of the online blog postings provided links to special offers and other content; therefore, URL links to the online versions are noted in each segment of this book for the reader's convenience. Readers may choose to copy and email certain URLs to colleagues.

We hope you will find this approach helpful for your professional efforts.

INTRODUCTION

"Each progressive spirit is opposed by a thousand men appointed to guard the past."
— Maurice Maeterlinck

Why another book on faculty development? Isn't that the question you're posing right now?

In the past few years of writing about faculty development, especially in our posts for New Forums Press' *Welcome Scholars* blog, we've found ourselves quoting Sorcinelli et al's impressive resource *Creating the Future of Faculty Development* (2006). Its title seems to hold more promise than Gillespie and Robertson's *A Guide to Faculty Development* (2010, 2nd ed.) as a go-to book since the latter is mainly sweeping, conceptual essays. Unfortunately, despite Sorcinelli's titular direction, the future, that future is upon us, and that book is now a decade old (as we go to press, we understand she is coming out with another book on the subject).

Are the main concerns of 2006 still the key issues of 2016? Using an extensive survey, Sorcinell reported that "Developers identified eight current issues they believed to be most important and that their programs currently address":

1. "Teaching for student-centered learning"
2. "New faculty development"
3. "Integrating technology into traditional teaching and learning settings"
4. "Active, inquiry-based, or problem-based learning"
5. "Assessing of student learning outcomes"
6. "Multiculturalism and diversity related to teaching"
7. "Scholarship of Teaching" and
8. "Writing Across the Curriculum" (pp. 71-72).

In our way of thinking, especially after watching some of our faculty developer colleagues across the country retire or return to their "first love" of teaching because their Center for Teaching and Learning (CTL) is being downsized or closed, the main issue facing the faculty development field is **SURVIVAL**. In an era of dwindling funding, how many universities both develop a strategic plan that prioritizes professional development (PD) and provide the funding to reach those goals?

Fortunately, however, faculty development programs have recently received new attention that might not only offer survival, but promote inclusion of these programs into the university's fabric. For example, Condon, Iverson, Manduca, Rutz, and Willett suggest that programs connect faculty learning with student learning (p. 8), which is the current model followed where we work at Eastern Kentucky University (EKU). The authors continue by arguing that faculty development influences teaching practices (p. 11) and that students benefit from innovative teaching techniques as shown by improved learning outcomes (p. 11). Thus, our own campus has focused its attention on the development of innovative teaching practices through its newly reshaped Teaching and Learning Innovation (TLI) series, Faculty Innovator program, and the Faculty Innovation Network. In addition, Rusty now chairs the University's Faculty Innovation Workgroup, focused on envisioning the future of professional development on campus. The workgroup recently reviewed Academic Impressions' *The State of Professional Development in Higher Education 2016* report, which found after a survey of 971 managers and frontline faculty and staff at colleges and universities "Evidence that institutions need to raise the bar of what they expect from professional development" (3). As higher education faces uncertain times, new ways of teaching and learning (or innovations in teaching and learning) will become more critical to the institution's mission, or as Academic Impressions summarized: "For these conversations, you will need ideas, fresh perspectives, and examples of how other institutions have innovated, and you need to seek these ideas outside the walls of your own institution. . . . [Institutions] will need to take new risks, pilot new ways of doing work, and challenge long-standing assumptions that may no longer apply" (p. 5).

In short, innovation in faculty development is mandatory not only for surviving but also thriving.

Institutions cannot rely on what they've done in the past or even the ways they've delivered faculty development content for their university colleagues. Thus, it's up to the creative-thinking scholars of teaching and learning and faculty development to introduce the path forward. This process will prompt faculty developers to reconsider the ways they're designing and administering content delivered face-to-face as well as online as our future system, currently in the development stages, suggests.

Whether you're interested in starting a faculty development program at your institution or reshaping one currently in place to make it more effective, the essays included in this book will point the way.

One of the first problems the book will address is one of vital concern to all faculty developers: trying to reach that majority of faculty who never attend PD events. If you can't entice faculty to come, what difference does it make whether you're discussing technology, the Scholarship of Teaching & Learning (SOTL), or multiculturalism? If Woody Allen is correct that 80% of success is just showing up, neither faculty developers nor faculty are successful.

Another problem we've found in faculty development is that traditional resources such as the aforementioned books tend to focus on general issues without getting into the nuts and bolts. We're tremendously interested in the details of faculty development—i.e., how the sausage is made. How do you deal with a provost? How do you stretch your budget? How should new faculty be best greeted their first day on campus? How can you create a state-wide conference to attract the best scholars to your campus? Taking inspiration from our highly successful New Forums Series, *It Works For Me*, we emphasized the practical in our essays. That is, we've approached issues from the perspective of our experience of a combined fifty years in faculty development.

Recently, Rusty became the new editor of the *Journal of Faculty Development*, and one of his first theme issues will deal with the future of faculty development. The three of us wrote the Call for Proposals and served as first readers. Why? To survive, faculty developers must focus on a future that may not even yet be on the horizon. What we've been reading excites us as we're finding essays that treat practical approaches to solving the problems that developers actually encounter on a daily basis.

As we've been writing our *Welcome Scholars* blog for the past two years, we find the greatest strength of the blog—and we write one 750-word post per week—is that it forces us to reflect in order to confront such a challenging future. This reflection has led to the successful implementation of some of our best ideas to transform faculty development on our campus. We want to share these strategies with you. You will note that the essays (for which we provide the dates they were posted) are not reprinted in chronological order, but are collected according to subject. As a result, a post will occasionally refer to another essay that will appear later in the book (or maybe not at all). These posts were written individually and not as chapters in a book; as a result you'll find that we have an intellectual core of principles derived from our favorite authors (including ourselves)—Gerry Nosich, Dee Fink, Mary Sorcinelli, and John Medina. Think of the repetition as embodiment of the principle of **Iteration**, something we discuss as part of **C.R.I.S.P.** (now you have to read on to find out for what the acronym stands).

Experienced researchers will note that dates rather than full citations are often provided for in-text references. Remember that the original posts tried to stay under 750 words. Anybody interested in the original source is invited to Google the author/title and read the book.

If nothing else, our aim is to stimulate a national conversation on how to build up this relatively new field of faculty development so as to be ready when the future collides with us. We've been through the "field wars" before—in creative writing and pop culture—so we know something about developing a body of research to help the field grow past respectability and legitimacy into a necessity. **The key is innovation**. Given a faculty population that looks upon professional development as a part of a Herculean workload with which they would rather not deal, dwindling funding not coming close to Dee Fink's 1% of total faculty (and adjunct and T.As) salaries ideal, and a student population changing very quickly and evermore falling behind in the learning gap, faculty development needs to be proactive, future-looking.

"Building a Culture of Innovation in Higher Education: Design & Practice for Leaders" (2015), a report created by a partnership of 2Revolutions and Educause, emphasizes that higher education is "moving from a culture of improvement focused on fixing current problems, to a culture of innovation that builds and tests new solutions" (p. 9) and offers the following definitions:

- **Innovation**: "the act or process of building on existing research, knowledge and practice through the introduction or application of new ideas, devices or methods to solve problems or create opportunities where none existed before";

By Charlie Sweet, Hal Blythe & Russell Carpenter

- **Culture of Innovation**: "Nurturing an environment that continually introduces new ideas or ways of thinking, then translates them into action to solve specific problems or seize new opportunities" (p. 8).

An underlying factor in the field's not gaining sufficient traction may be the unwillingness to take what Academic Impressions calls "intelligent risks." Risks cost money, whether they bring about dismal failures or splendid successes, and we've just said dwindling funding is a problem. So is an administration that seems fundamentally risk-averse and a burdened faculty not willing to take on one more straw. In order to meet the challenge, faculty developers—let's call them **Faculty Innovators**—will need a set of creativity-based skills we wrote about in our *Introduction to Applied Creative Thinking* (2012) as the **Nifty Nine**:
- Shifting Perception
- Piggybacking
- Brainstorming
- Glimmer-Catching
- Collaborating
- Going with the Flow
- Playing
- Recognizing Pattern
- Using Metaphor

Innovating faculty development can be done with these skills. It must be done. And in the following pages, we're going to demonstrate how. The book's first section contains essays addressing the fundamental theories underlying creative thinking and then its application to faculty development, while the following sections treat practical concerns. For these pedagogical essays, we often include a set of ancillaries to aid you in reflecting about and implementing the strategies presented. While we have created an extensive approach to innovating faculty development, we encourage you to take a risk and attempt a few of them at first. If those innovations succeed, feel free to keep borrowing more and more from our suggestions. They work for us.

References

Academic Impressions. (2016). *The State of Professional Development in Higher Education*. Retrieved 25 February 2015 from http://www.academicimpressions.com

Condon, William, Ellen R. Iverson, Cathryn A. Manduca, Carol Rutz, and Gudrun Willet. (2016). *Faculty Development and Student Learning: Assessing the Connections*. Bloomington, IN: IU Press.

Sweet, Charlie, Russell Carpenter, Hal Blythe, and Shawn Apostel. (2013). *Teaching Applied Creative Thinking: A New Pedagogy for the 21st Century*. Stillwater, OK: New Forums Press.

2Revolutions and Educause. (2015). "Building a Culture of Innovation in Higher Education:Design & Practice for Leaders." Retrieved 12 July 2016 from http://net.educause.edu/ir/library/pdf/NGT1502.pdf

FOUNDATIONAL THEORY

A. The Importance of Creative Thinking to Academia's Future

1. Why Successful Faculty Development Requires Innovation

(Posted 28 July 2015)

http://newforums.com/?s=Why+Successful+Faculty+Development+Requires+Innovation

Is the term "innovative faculty development" actually redundant? In our way of thinking faculty development, mostly because of its youth, necessitates innovation. In fact, any new field depends upon creative thinking and its implementation into innovation to progress. During our academic careers, despite a background in traditional studies in English, we have helped develop three new disciplines—pop culture (especially comic book theory), creative writing, and now faculty development. Our careers have coincided with the rise of these three fields as they, like us, got their start in the 1960s.

But here we want to focus on faculty development. While the more formal structure we think of as faculty development began around 50 years ago, way back in 1810 Harvard University granted its first sabbatical, and many claim that action as the first instance of faculty development. In *Creating the Future of Faculty Development* (2006), Sorcinelli et al posit that faculty development has evolved through five ages:

- The Age of the Scholar (1960s-mid 70s)
- The Age of the Teacher (mid-to-late 70s)
- The Age of the Developer (1980s)
- The Age of the Learner (1990s), and
- The Age of the Network (21st century).

Obviously such constant change necessitates innovation.

In his "Afterword" to the second edition of Gillespie and Robertson's *A Guide to Faculty Development* (2010), William Bergquist describes this fifty-year growth as "The Diffusion of Faculty Development as an Innovation" (406). Bergquist also identifies four factors that have made faculty development "respectable and acceptable on college and university campuses":

1. "building a base of research evidence and interdisciplinary scholarship"
2. "constructing solid administrative support"
3. "building upon newly emerging institutional norms and values" and
4. "establishing a profession to guide the further development of the field" (409).

In short, the basic nature of a new field is change, and through innovation faculty development has sustained its progress. Interestingly, the Subject Index to Gillespie and Robertson's book contains no heading for either "Innovation" or "Creative Thinking" as the assumption seems to be that these two concepts have provided the field's firm foundation for fifty years.

And innovation will continue to undergird the maturation of faculty development because of the constant changing of higher education itself. Several forces are causing centers for teaching and learning (CTLs) to adapt. In fact, the term CTL is a bit misleading as every CTL we know is slightly different in terms of size, budget, composition, reporting responsibility, and mission. In our own short fifteen year history, for example, we have gone from a pure faculty-facing unit, lost our control of the university's IT division, and recently merged with a student-facing studio for academic creativity. Innovate or perish has been our unofficial motto.

Change abounds for all CTLs. Due to the spiraling cost of higher education, many centers have been closed/funding has been cut. Other forces providing challenges have been identified by Gillespie and Robertson's book by Lee:
- Sophistication of learning technologies
- Diversification and globalization of the student body
- Ascendance of assessment
- Networking (Sorcinelli's term)—i.e., being asked to partner with internal and external units
- "Adjuncting" of CTL clientele: many institutions report over half of the professorate is part-time (30)
- Additional responsibilities.

Let's investigate the last item on the list. We often joke that the "L" in TLC (the Teaching & Learning Center) actually stands for "landfill." Each year we are "asked" to take on additional work (and, no, the budget never seems to increase). For instance, while we have always been in charge of New Faculty Orientation, recently we have picked up Part-Time Orientation and T.A. Training. This year we added the training of instructors in the First-Year Courses program. When the Provost's Professional Development Series (i.e., putting on a major workshop such as Dee Fink's Creating Significant Learning Experiences) was instituted two years ago, we made the arrangements.

Faculty development also has to respond to changing realities. For instance, faculty across the country are being asked to do more, while simultaneously research shows that new faculty treat professing less as a calling and more as a 9:00 to 5:00 job. As a CTL, we are still tasked with developing these time-taxed professionals, but how do we do it? Certainly, the traditional lunch-and-learn session has lost its luster. That sounds like a post for next time.

2. How to Weave Creative Thinking into the Institutional Fabric

(Posted 30 September 2014)

http://newforums.com/weave-creative-thinking-institutional-fabric/

When we were researching creative thinking for both our *Introduction to Applied Creative Thinking* (2012) and our *Teaching Applied Creative Thinking* (2013), we ran across an interesting detail. How many courses focused on developing applied creative thinking in universities across the world—in Asia, the Americas, and Europe—do you think actually exist? According to Xu et al (2005), only 39 such courses are on the books, and the bulk of them are isolated in departments and not tied to any specific program, major, or minor. Similarly, our research into universities offering minors in creativity back in those dark ages showed only one university even offering a master's degree in creative thinking.

Given the popularity of insightful books such as Florida's *The Rise of the Creative Class* (2002), McWilliam's *The Creative Workforce* (2008), and Pink's *A Whole New Mind* (2005) as well as the IBM report (2010) that creative thinking was the number-one skill American CEOs wanted from college graduates, we expected more. More courses, more programs, more colleges and universities responding to a need and a desire.

For the past four years our institution's catalog has contained our Minor in Applied Creating Thinking, and we're pretty certain in the nine years since Xu *et al* report that other schools have likewise responded with courses, minors, and programs. If that isn't the case, however, and you are interested in weaving applied creative thinking into your institution's curricula, how might you go about that task?

One, <u>consider responding to your accrediting agency</u>. Our mode of attack early in the twenty-first century came to us when we discovered that our university's accrediting agency, SACS, was insisting institutions implement a new accreditation piece, the Quality Enhancement Program (QEP), a sort of value-added academic piece. We insinuated our way onto the University's QEP committee and helped steer the discussion toward creative thinking. As a result, in 2007 the institution declared as its QEP theme that it would "develop [later graduate] informed critical and creative thinkers who communicate effectively."

Two, since every QEP needs a home, <u>consider what type of organization will be needed to support the QEP</u>. Here, EKU launched the Noel Studio for Academic Creativity, the centerpiece of the university community and hub of communication and creative activity. It houses the Minor in Applied Creative Thinking and annually hosts programs for members of the university community.

Three, <u>utilize professional learning communities.</u> As soon as our QEP was instituted, the University created QEP Coaches, who helped train the faculty in critical thinking. As creative thinking was being neglected, we started a campus-wide professional learning community (PLC) with twelve faculty members. This PLC was tasked with researching creative initiatives and suggesting ways to encourage creative thinking across our campus. Because of the unique structure of the PLC, we were able to permeate the campus community (both academic and social) with creative endeavors.

Four, <u>create a course</u>. When we taught creative writing, we developed all sorts of courses on the subject, from Teaching Creative Writing to Becoming a Professional Writer. Invention is such an important concept in writing that it would have been a natural, but alas, we never worked on it. For our creative thinking initiative, we decided to lead off with a course introducing the concept and treating the basics of implementation. We named the course Introduction to Applied Creative Thinking and even wrote its textbook built on our years of research and application in the field. The success of this initial class has led to the creation of several additional courses designed specifically for the minor, including its capstone course.

Five, <u>develop extant courses on creativity into a minor</u>. When we facilitated our PLC, we found various faculty were teaching courses related to creativity. One member was teaching a course in business that we tried to appropriate. Another member had a friend teaching a Creative Collaboration course in Psychology, and still another taught the College of Education's Gifted and Talented course.

Six, <u>tie to extant or developing programs</u>. Last year the University found that a significant number of students were not finishing up their degree when they were less than 30 hours from graduation. At the same time another task force zeroed in on our extended campuses (we have ten regional appendices) that were unable to offer outlying populations enough majors. As a result of these two problems, a Bachelor of General Studies degree was created, but it needed some core courses. Of course, we suggested that Introduction to Applied Creative Thinking provided skills desired by employers in all fields. We have also tied our introductory course, CRE 101, to a capstone program in the University's College of Justice and Safety.

Where do we go from here? If the minor does well, maybe we need to transform it into a major. Perhaps the creativity initiatives developed on campus should extend to the community or local schools. Or maybe creativity programs will find a home online.

3. Using Creative Thinking to Innovate Faculty Development

(Posted 6 April 2016)

http://newforums.com/?s=Using+Creative+Thinking+to+Innovate+Faculty+Development

What is the relationship between innovation and faculty development? In the past we have discussed it in the abstract, but this time we'd like to demonstrate how being able to employ creative thinking effectively provides centers of teaching and learning (CTLs) with a huge advantage over non-users.

The General Problem

For the past few years we have been offering various programs—noted speakers, workshops, and professional learning communities—to help the faculty with non-disciplinary professional development in primarily pedagogy, technology, and scholarship. Over the years, through experience and research, we have learned some valuable lessons. One, one-shots (e.g., a PowerPoint presentation on how a faculty member flipped her classroom) don't have long-lasting value. Two, faculty feel so time-constrained by all their responsibilities that they find it difficult to attend CTL sessions they admit would be helpful.

The Process Begins

The problem, then, demands a solution that ensures continuity and delivery. For that solution, we started with something we had written about in our *Introduction to Applied Creative Thinking* (New Forums, 2012), creative thinking strategies—**Collaborations** involving **Brainstorming** sessions with the three of us (Charlie, Hal, and Rusty), our Faculty Innovators, and a representative campus group. An early revelation was that professional development, like detergents in your washing machine, is best delivered through concentration, but the major insight was the need for an online professional development system (OPDS).

Through **Pattern Recognition,** the campus group eventually figured out that video-gaming provided an excellent model for professional development. Faculty could proceed up a hierarchy of four levels, progressing from Learner to Practitioner to Advocate to Scholar. Each level offered not only complexity, but roughly paralleled Bloom's Taxonomy. Now, since all faculty need differing areas of development, we began the system by developing four-level modules in Flipping the Classroom, the Scholarship of Teaching and Learning, Critical and Creative Thinking, and the Foundations of Pedagogy. Later, when the workgroup decided it needed a test module, it selected a basic, hot-button issue on campus, metacognition, which meant we had to create a fifth module.

The Stumbling Block

Creating the four-level metacognition module appeared relatively easy at first. After all, one of our group members, Matt (also our Faculty Innovators Coordinator), had developed a template for the first module, Flipping the Classroom, which meant essentially we just followed the template. As we built the module and prepared to hand it off to an instructional designer who would translate it to our campus course management system, Blackboard, however, we stumbled. Reading over what we had written and essentially kept on replicating didn't make sense. We started asking unanswerable questions such as:

- What is the rationale for this OPDS?
- What kind of directions should a user follower?
- How would the faculty user submit abstracts, analyses, and applications of the fundamental and powerful concepts found in the modules' basic readings and videos?

The Solution—A Creative Thinking Strategy

The solution was as close as a copy of our *Introduction to Applied Creative Thinking*. One of our so-called Nifty Nine creative thinking strategies was **Perception Shift**, which we claimed "involves looking at a person, idea, or situation from a new perspective" (p. 28). Essentially, our problem revolved around our thinking of professional development from the point of view of a professional developer, so what we had to do was shift our perspective to that of a faculty user.

Faculty needed to be provided with a rationale for taking up their busy time. They also had to be given explicit directions on how to use the OPDS, and the system had to be simple enough for them to use while complex enough to be useful. Again, we harkened back to the key definition that a creative idea had to be both **novel** and **useful**.

Just as authors occasionally switch the point of view so that key situations are apprehended from a different perspective, we found that as soon as we worked on the module from the point of view of the user, the module seemed to write itself. Thinking as a user, we asked ourselves what information faculty members would most like to possess at key junctures in the module. What questions would they ask? We even decided that providing a video guide on the side for the faculty member offered many advantages.

Conclusion

The irony is that we began as creative writers, and even as faculty developers we wrote quite a few books in New Forums' "ACT Creativity Series," yet when the going got tough, we almost forgot what we had written.

4. Tuesday Mornings

(to be published)

Psst, want to know a secret? We'll basically go anywhere across campus and meet with anybody—administrator, faculty, or student—at any time. Except for one block. Tuesday morning from 8:30-10:00. Do you know why Tuesday is sacred?

Every time we do a collective presentation, workshop, class, or similar meeting, when the Q&A begins, we can absolutely predict the first two questions:
- How do you guys work together so well?
- Where do you guys get your ideas?

We'd like to answer both questions because for the most part the answer is the same as this post's teaser. Tuesday mornings.

For the past three years, the three of us (one editor of ours calls us the "Kentucky Trio") meet, usually **in the same place**--Hal and Charlie's office except some summer days on the adjoining veranda. **At the same time**, 8:30. We begin slowly with coffee, donuts, and small sports talk, usually about our *alma maters* (by pure coincidence, each of us received a degree from a different institution of higher learning in Florida, so we have a starting point in common). The major point is that we are both organized and disciplined.

After a few minutes one of us, usually Charlie, pulls out an **agenda**, a list of key topics he has been keeping on his desk since our last meeting. The agenda has at least three items as we work under the same directive as TV soaps. A Hollywood writer once told us you make a soap opera the way a chef makes a three-course meal on the stove; you have three plots at three different stages: one you are just starting to mix, one you are heating up, and one you are bringing to a boil. Usually we start talking about the project nearing completion. For instance, last week we had to prepare a final draft for a program we call Faculty Innovators, and it had to be proofread as well as supplied with a better last step.

We then move to something we are in the middle of. Normally, we're writing two or three things simultaneously—blog posts, articles, books, or a basic academic document. While we have never **assigned roles**, we have discovered that like Liam Neeson in the *Taken* movie franchise, each of us is a man with "a very particular set of skills." Charlie, for instance, is best at starting a piece and working with its big ideas/fundamental and powerful concepts. Hal has mastered the close reading for organizational, stylistic, and mechanical problems. Rusty excels at research, from finding the arcane detail to putting a citation in a proper format (in our work we find we use three different citation styles).

But the segment of each session we live for is the one we postpone for the very reason that if we started with burner #1, we'd never get to burner # 2 or 3. Brainstorming. While we have researched and written extensively about the process, we don't have any formal ideas for coming up with the next project, paper, column, campus responsibility. However, if we were to be metacognitive, here are some of the **guidelines** that influence our brainstorming:

- Come to each meeting with at least one idea you have begun to shape.
- Be willing to bring up any idea--no matter how trivial, undeveloped, or poor you think it is. As we say in *Introduction to Applied Creative Thinking* (2012), learn to catch glimmers as well as more-developed ideas.
- Let all ideas live for a while.
- Listen and jot down the best of what you hear.
- Once an idea is out, rather than evaluating it, piggyback/build on it.
- Develop the idea far enough so that each person has an understanding of what we are talking about.
- Assess the idea as to whether it needs to be deleted, saved in our parking lot (actually a file), or further developed.
- Choose one person to write up the embryo of the idea into an introductory paragraph. That writing is sometimes passed around the following session as burner #2, but more often than not, we can't wait until next Tuesday, so we have been circulating the idea by email drafts or using Dropbox or Google Drive to work on it.
- Assume collaborative ownership. Here's some inside baseball. When we send a post to our editor, we are usually asked who wrote it. The truth is that by the time the idea is sent out, we all own it and rarely can we look at a finished product and remember who wrote what, so the posts get published in alphabetical order.

Unfortunately, 10:00 comes to Tuesday mornings all too quickly. Meetings end with us in the middle of our game, not because we have run out of ideas with which to play ping pong. Now you know our secret—regular time, regular place, regular process—and the discipline to do it each week.

B. Applying Creative Thinking to Faculty Development

By Charlie Sweet, Hal Blythe & Russell Carpenter

1. How Design Thinking Helps Innovate Faculty Development, Part I

(Posted 20 April 2016)

http://newforums.com/how-design-thinking-helps-innovate-faculty-development-part-i/

Throughout the years in our center for teaching & learning (CTL), we've pretty much relied on our own approach to creative thinking, something we've discussed in these posts but really detailed in *Introduction to Applied Creative Thinking* (2012) and *Teaching Applied Creative Thinking* (2013). Recently, to help guide us through numerous projects, we've been using another form of creative thinking called Design Thinking, adapting it to suit our purposes. Beginning as a business approach, design thinking has found its way into education from K-12 to higher ed, and it's a process you might want to look into.

Design Thinking Defined

According to Tim Brown, CEO and president of IDEO (an innovation and design firm), design thinking is "a methodology that imbues the full spectrum of innovation activities with a human-centered design ethos. By this, I mean innovation is powered by a thorough understanding, through direct observation of what people want and need in their lives and what they like or dislike about the way particular products are made, packaged, marketed, sold, and supported" (p. 86). As professional developers, what interested us most is Brown's proclamation that "innovation's terrain is expanding. Its objectives are no longer just physical products; they are new sorts of processes, services, IT-powered interactions, entertainments, and ways of communicating and collaborating" (p. 86).

At its foundation design thinking is a transferrable process. Depending on your source, design thinking has various stages:

- Seven Stage: define, research, ideate, prototype, choose, implement, and learn
- Five Stage: Redefining the problem, need-finding and benchmarking, ideating, building, and testing
- Stanford dschool: empathize, define, ideate (brainstorm), prototype, test (seeking feedback)—acronymically **EDIPT**
- Brown's Three-Space/Three I Approach: inspiration, ideation, and implementation.

Why Design Thinking

O.K., you say, but why do we need design thinking? Can't we just use our traditional approaches, such as SWOT (Strengths, Weaknesses, Opportunities, and Threats) analysis, or rational problem-solving?

First, some situations manifest what Rittel (1973) refers to as **wicked problems,** wherein it's difficult to discern the problem much less the solution. Such situations are not wicked in the sense of evil, but rather an ill-defined rat's nest.

Second, traditional rational analysis does not necessarily begin with the human-centeredness of the problem. In academia students and faculty take center stage in our deliberations.

Third, rational problem-solving techniques are not necessarily collaborative, whereas design thinking depends upon a group. Collaborations increase ideation levels and provide multiple perspectives on the same situation being studied.

Fourth, rational problem-solving tends to be linear, whereas design thinking encourages recursiveness. As Brown explains about the three spaces—inspiration, ideation, and implementation—"Projects will loop back through these spaces—particularly the first two—more than once as ideas are refined and new directions taken" (p. 89).

Fifth, design thinking is fun. It focuses on a human-centered situation, and it employs a human-centered approach to deal with the situation. Therefore, design thinking satisfies the humans involved in the situation as well as those of the group examining the situation. Brown believes that "Often the emotional connection to a product or an image is what engages us in the first place" (p. 92). In *A Whole New Mind* (2008) Pink labelled this concept "high touch."

Sixth, proper implementation of design thinking often provides not one solution (per rational analysis) but several. All solutions can be tried, and not every one will be successful or the proper fit for each individual.

Seventh, design thinking is applicable to many situations, and, most importantly, it's not just reserved for business.

Conclusion

Design thinking is a sort of intellectual Leatherman tool that can be applied to higher education in many ways, and here are some:
- Curricula redesign
- A curriculum in itself
- Ascertaining the role of evolving technologies
- Examining learning space
- Problem-solving of any subject
- An alternative to the right-wrong constriction of student learning often found in testing.

Does design thinking have limitations? Certainly users must be trained. Users must get beyond the K-12 bubble-in testing mentality. Some problems can be reduced to the algebraic x=?. And not everyone is comfortable using such an approach.

Next time we'll take you through some instances where we have practiced design thinking, breaking the process down to its stages and using very real examples.

References

Brown, T. (2008, June). Design thinking. *Harvard Business Review*, 84-92.

Pink, D. (2005). *A whole new mind*. New York: Riverhead Books.

Rittel, H., & Webber, M. (1973). Dilemmas in a general theory of planning. *Policy Sciences, 4*(2), 155-169.

2. How Design Thinking Helps Innovate Faculty Development, Part II

(Posted 27 April 2016)
http://newforums.com/?s=How+Design+Thinking+Helps+Innovate+Faculty+Development%2C+Part+II

In *The Ten Faces of Innovation* (2008), Tom Kelley, general manager of the design firm IDEO, emphasizes the essence of design theory's philosophy of rapid experimentation by citing an old IDEO maxim: "Fail often, to succeed sooner" (p. 52). Hopefully, last week's Part I on the relationship between faculty development and design thinking made clear the importance of risk. In Part II, we'd like to provide some examples of how we've been using design thinking to drive our new and experimental program we've mentioned in earlier posts, our Faculty Innovators. Without our taking that risk back then, the program would not be almost a year old now.

The Faculty Innovators Program as Example

The very existence of the Faculty Innovators program offers a testament to design thinking. To create the Faculty Innovators, the three of us basically followed the process we described in the last post as employed by Stanford's dschool (design school) of EDIPT: **E**mpathize, **D**efine, **I**deate, **P**rototype, and **T**est.

Empathize: to develop a new method of professional development that was definitely not the traditional PD programming of a center for teaching & learning, we started by discussing what we would have wanted as help both back in the day and currently. Hal and Charlie taught English for 37 years before going over to the dark side of administration. Rusty, on the other hand, is both a faculty member (in English) and an administrator (of our Noel Studio for Academic Creativity). One answer dominated the conversation: help is more easily accepted when it comes from one's peers, not administrators. Whether it's that sense of independence or dislike of being told what to do (often expressed as "academic freedom"), faculty like to feel that after a minimum of nine years of college and being in the one-half of one percent who hold Ph.D.s, they can solve problems themselves. Therefore, we had to have a program with faculty helping faculty.

Define: We needed a professional development program that not only gained acceptance, but possessed key pedagogical knowledge, skills, and strategies. Hence, we settled on Faculty Innovators (FIs).

Ideate: Before descending on our dean with our latest scheme, for over a semester we brainstormed the key aspects of the proposed program. How would we select FIs? How would we compensate them? How would we train them? How often? What would our organizational chart look like? Where would we meet? What kind of services would we offer? Most importantly for an administrator's ears, we had to project a cost. What we quickly realized is that we could not define everything we needed—we were taking a great risk.

Prototype: Despite not having a perfectly developed and polished program in our hands, last spring we went to our dean with our proposal. We agreed that we would reallocate our funds for the program if she would aid by providing for the reassigned time for our Faculty Innovator Coordinator. We also agreed that the three of us would act as the Executive Committee without any extra compensation and that we would make time to make the program work. She signed off on the program, and we start recruiting the best faculty we could find with at least one from each of the University's six colleges.

Test: This past academic year we have been not only testing the program, but refining it as we go. For instance, in the beginning FI meetings were held every two weeks, but changed to every three weeks, and each academic year each FI would 1) facilitate one professional learning community and 2) put on one workshop in our Teaching & Learning Innovations Series. Meetings began with two-minute reports from each FI, and each meeting had a mini-training on some key aspect. Along the way, we have kept records of who attended what activity, sent out evaluation forms to participants after workshops, and maintained records of consultations and observations. We meet in three weeks to develop an assessment report of year one for our dean.

A Concluding Example

In two earlier posts, "An Inside Look at a Faculty Innovator's Progress" (February 3, 2016) and "An Inside Look at The Faculty Innovator Progress" (February 11, 2016), we offered a peek at what we actually do during a progress (what most people call a "retreat"). We even described how we paired the FIs into teams to develop outlines of video modules and "create a low-res prototype that embodied the essence of their module."

We didn't mention it to them then (nor did we refer to it in the two aforementioned columns), but what we were providing our FIs were some exercises, some on-the-job training in design thinking. In fact, we didn't really bring up (or even use the name) the concept of design thinking (our FIs have been overwhelmed as it is) until this week when we passed out an article by Tom Brown, CEO and president of IDEO, on "Design Thinking" (2008) that appeared in the *Harvard Business Review*.

Yes, one of our early goals was to be <u>intentional</u> in the presentation of design thinking, but we took the <u>risk</u> of explaining it to them after they had actually been using it for a while. Putting them through the process a few times, we believe, has made their acceptance of the process greater and their understanding of it deeper.

Now you have an insight into our <u>pedagogy of faculty development</u> as well as our program. Parts of our faculty innovator program may fail, but the essence of the program will not only survive but be successful because we followed Tom Kelley's advice and took a big risk.

3. The Faculty Developer's Most Important Question

(Posted 13 July 2016)

http://newforums.com/the-faculty-developers-most-important-question/

To write *Creating the Future of Faculty Development* (2006), Sorcinelli *et al* sent out an 18-question survey to a host of faculty developers—e.g., what kind of institution is yours, what are your program goals and purposes, and what services do you currently offer? To our way of thinking, the surveyors omitted the key question.

If you are a director of a center for teaching and learning (CTL) at your institution, what would you consider the single most important question to ask in your position? And for bonus points, to whom would you address this question? Actually, knowing the answer to the latter question should help you tackle the former.

While you're thinking, we'd like to tell you an anecdote. At the beginning of the summer, we wanted to do some research on CTLs in states contiguous to Kentucky, so we wrote some friends who serve as CTL directors for help. One very old friend wrote back, regretting she could not help because she had been removed as center director. Her plight is one of the reasons we decided to write on this topic.

In truth, this key question was suggested to us by our original discipline. All three of us started our careers as instructors in English, and one of the basic rhetorical principles instilled in us in graduate school was the principle of audience. Every time you write, you don't just write per se, you address a particular audience; and that singular or plural entity determines everything from your style to your word choice, to your degree of formality or informality to the type and amount of evidence you employ. Emailing an old friend, for instance, places different demands on you than writing a piece of educational research or a spec script for *The Walking Dead*.

Now, our answer. The most important question for us you as a faculty developer is: **to whom do you report**? Why? Because none of the other questions or answers about what you think may matter at all. What matters most is what matters most to your boss.

A case in point comes from an old friend, Dee Fink, who has written an essay "Innovative Ways of Assessing Faculty Development" (2013). In the article Dee discusses various ways to assess faculty development that take the assessor beyond attendance and satisfaction. While Dee really does offer some innovative assessments, he doesn't confront what for us is the key reason for the assessments.

What does your boss want from you? If your boss is a basic bean-counter who thrives on reports that offer the number of faculty participants, it doesn't make sense to provide satisfaction surveys using the psychometric Likert scale, faculty testimonials to what was learned during CTL sessions, or even how individual faculty implemented what they learned.

We once had the owner of the local McDonald's tell us that customers come in looking for hamburger, so he doesn't feed them steak. Actually, that was then, and McSteak and McLobster can now be found seasonally at regional McDonald's.

Which brings up another important guideline. While you give your boss what s/he wants, nothing is wrong with supplying a little additional information (like student reflections on techniques Professor X learned in your flipping the classroom workshop) just as long as you also provide the hamburger.

In previous posts we have described how we have a weekly Tuesday morning meeting. What we haven't mentioned is that we also have monthly meetings with our boss, the dean of University Programs. Our Tuesday morning agendas usually contain some information about a meeting or other communication with her that we need to work on. For instance, as the University just came out with a new five-year strategic plan, we were told to rewrite our unit's last plan so as to align with that of the University.

Simultaneously, we have been busy gently nudging our dean to urge her boss to move toward a required professional development plan for each faculty member. Nudging is good, but unless you provide the basic hamburger, you might not be around to serve much longer.

4. Applying Pedagogy as the Fifth Creative Thinking Perspective

(Posted 15 June 2016)

http://newforums.com/applying-pedagogy-fifth-creative-thinking-perspective/

Hasn't the time come for creative thinking researchers to begin a scholarly conversation about the fifth P? What, you didn't realize there were already four Ps?

In our *Introduction To Applied Creative Thinking* (2012), we explain that since Rhodes (1965) "creative thinking theorists tend to regard the field from four different perspectives, commonly called the Four Ps":

- The Creative **Process** "consists of those learned skills that innovative thinkers employ."
- The Creative **Person** "is the focus of studies that examine those personality traits that produce a creative thinker."
- The Creative **Press** "is a term used to describe the environment that contributes to optimal creativity."
- The Creative **Product** is "the end result of the previous Ps—did the process, press, and person produce something tangible that is useful?" (pp. 2-4).

For us the fifth P is **pedagogy**, which Holberg and Taylor (2005) define as "incarnational teaching, that is, the embodiment of principles in practice." Perhaps we believe in the importance of pedagogy because we have spent our careers in higher education, most recently focusing on professional development, or maybe it's simply that we subscribe to the old adage that you don't completely know something until you can teach it to someone else. No matter the source of our belief, we have noticed the past few years as we review the literature on applied creative thinking that too few researchers try to answer the question, "How can I utilize all these insights into creativity in my teaching?"

Stated in other terms, we are vitally concerned with how to transform our students into creative thinkers. So far, our response has been twofold. First, we developed an 18-hour Minor in Applied Creative Thinking wherein students begin the minor with CRE 101 Introduction to Applied Creative Thinking and complete the minor with a capstone course. The other 12 hours can be fulfilled by students taking various creativity courses in specific disciplines (e.g., psych, education, business) or within the minor (e.g., an innovation course, a course into creativity research, and even a course in teaching the subject). And to provide continuity between the courses, as well as a common vocabulary, we have written the aforementioned *Introduction To Applied Creative Thinking* (2012) and *Teaching Applied Creative Thinking* (2013).

So what do we think should be done to bring the fifth P, pedagogy, into the spotlight?

One, as we alluded to earlier, <u>researchers need to explore how creative strategies are best taught</u>. For instance, we just (8 January 2014) checked the *Creativity Research Journal* website (<u>http://www.tandfonline.com/action/showMostReadArticles?journalCode=hcrj20#.VK63FV5ASUk</u>) that lists their "ten most read articles," and not one of them is focused on pedagogy. Interestingly, we wrote *Teaching Applied Creative Thinking* because we could not find a suitable textbook in that area.

Second, <u>graduate schools need a greater emphasis on pedagogy</u>—not just the pedagogy of creativity, but pedagogy in general, but that's another column . . . if not book.

Third, <u>faculty members need to think about how to include creative thinking in their classes</u>. Nobody we know has executed a search of America's colleges and universities aimed at discovering how many classes have goals/student learning outcomes centered on creative thinking. And even if more higher ed faculty included such learning goals, would the students receive enough K-12 training in creative thinking to be ready for this approach?

Fourth, and perhaps most important, <u>the academy needs to admit that such a thing as the scholarship of creativity exists</u>. After all, if you check Boyer's seminal *Scholarship Reconsidered* (1990), you'll find four categories of scholarship listed—discovery, integration, application, and teaching (what we now call the scholarship of teaching and learning)--and not one of them is the scholarship of creativity. We applaud Boyer's emphasis on teaching, but 25 years ago, despite his rationale that the traditional definition of scholarship needed to be broadened to include social and environmental changes, the scholarship of creativity did not even receive a footnote. We often feel lucky that we work at a university that for almost half a century has recognized what it calls the "scholarship of creative endeavor." Nonetheless, most people in higher ed don't recognize that such a scholarship exists, and the few who do would be hard pressed to define it, come up with a rationale, or provide a research process that falls into this category.

Ultimately the pedagogy of creativity will not exist until the scholarship of creativity is developed, so get researching!

5. Creating Unified Higher Ed Faculty Development Programming

(Posted December 30, 2015)

http://newforums.com/creating-unified-higher-ed-faculty-development-programming/

In *Learning To Think Things Through* (2005), Gerry Nosich claims that every course needs a focus, what he calls "the central question . . . It is the unifying question, and everything in the course fits into that question" (111). In every literature course we teach, for instance, we have two **central questions** that we choose to formulate in the form of declarative sentences:
- Art reflects the culture that produces it.
- What differentiates art from nature is art has unity, and in literature every element—plot, character, setting, method of narration, and imagery—contributes to that unity or it doesn't belong.

Unified Faculty Development

Faculty development programming, likewise, needs a central concern—be it a question or declaration—around which it revolves. Why? Research demonstrates that isolated one-shot presentations have little effect on the faculty. In actuality--as we pointed out in "What Services Should a CTL Offer?"--we divide all our CTL efforts into three types of programming—orientations, informational roundtables, and pedagogical workshops. With the exception of informational roundtables (e.g., how the counselling center works, what you need to know about disabilities and accommodations), the rest of our programming follows a unified approach. Just as iteration reinforces central concerns in courses, so that principle applies to CTLs.

How do we achieve this unity? Every CTL needs both guiding values and annual themes. Our guiding value is encapsulated in our motto "Helping Teachers Help Students Learn Deeply," which aligns well with our unit's (the Noel Studio) chief objective, deep student learning. This year's major theme at the University as initiated by our provost is metacognition, so we have developed workshops and professional learning communities around that subject.

Milestone Events

The chief way we create a unified program is through a series of **milestone events**—i.e., major programming. Milestone events are held each year and spaced out through two semesters. Faculty members rely on their existence and plan their annual professional development programs around these events. We embed the major theme in all these events. Each year we start out with four milestone events, aiming to run two per semester:

1. <u>Orientations</u> (i.e., New Faculty, Part-Time, First-Year Courses Instructors, and Teaching Assistants): held in August before the actual start of the fall semester, these workshops introduce new instructors to the basics of becoming a successful professor.

2. <u>Provost's Speaker Series</u> (e.g., metacognition this year, significant learning experi-

ences last year): chosen by the provost with consultation from our unit, this event brings in a nationally known expert to address the faculty (and occasionally students) through a lecture/workshop.

 3. <u>Scholarship Week</u>: held in April, this week-long event celebrates and showcases both faculty and student scholarship with displays, speakers, and workshops.

 4. <u>Pedagogicon</u>: held every May, this pedagogical conference started a few years ago as the Kentucky Pedagogicon, but is now increasing its participation range. This year's theme is "Exploring High-Impact Educational Practices Using Scholarly and Creative Teaching."

Other Events Developing Our Unified Themes

 Not all faculty members are new, so attending even three events does not provide sufficient pedagogical development. Throughout the year, we also offer other ways to reinforce the academic year's fundamental and powerful concepts, some of which we have discussed in prior blogs: classroom observations, individual consultations, workshops, and communities--i.e., professional learning communities, Breakfast and a Books, creative communities.

 In addition, we have this year implemented two experimental programs that we will explain in future blogs. Essentially, these new initiatives stem from the recognition that today's faculty differ from that of even a decade ago. These newly minted profs consider teaching a 9-5 job, revere technology, and are more likely than not teaching one or more online classes. As a result, they expect training to come to them.

 The **Faculty Innovators** initiative is an approach whereby the most effective faculty are selected, trained, and then sent back to the colleges, departments, and programs to put on workshops and provide consultations.

 The Faculty Innovator Network is basically a technological resource, offering videos on important topics (e.g., student demographics at our university, how to get started publishing, an intro to metacognition).

 But the key to every activity we sponsor, provide, and support is unity—somehow each one aims at transforming our students into deep learners.

6. Resources on Unifying Faculty Development Programming

(Posted 23 March 2016)

http://newforums.com/resources-unifying-higher-ed-faculty-development-programming/

 A few posts ago we discussed the importance of a center for teaching & learning (CTL) developing unified programming—i.e., a central concern around which it revolves. We even made the comment that "Research demonstrates that isolated one-shot presentations have little effect on the faculty." For those of you wondering about that research, we have a major source for you, and we have an elaboration beyond the previous suggestion of milestone events for creating unity.

Key Research

William Condon, Ellen Iverson, Cathryn Manduca, Carol Rutz, and Gudrun Willet recently published *Faculty Development and Student Learning: Assessing the Connections* (Bloomington: Indiana University Press, 2016) that focuses on developing the golden link between programming offered by CTLs, the faculty absorbing that knowledge, and the resulting increase in student learning. Performing the research at Carleton College and Washington State University, the authors claim, "the research process led to the conclusion that the single workshop is not the correct unit of measure. The ethnographic and interview data clearly show the interaction of multiple workshops over time" (58). And the faculty subject concurred with that conclusion: "Faculty professed to like events that had their priorities straight—meaning events that faculty perceived as focused on important aspects of teaching. They tended to dislike events that were required or that they perceived as addressing more trivial topics, such as learning to use the new course management software. Faculty valued initiatives that provided support and that were iterative in nature" (127).

Possible Application

One way to create this unity and iteration is through theming. Each CTL can craft a central motif around which much of the academic year's faculty development programming can revolve—milestone events, presentations, and communities.

As we have stated previously, much of our early programming, especially in the fall, was really just an extension of New Faculty Orientation (NFO), offering campus shops that had no time to present their services during NFO an opportunity. Thus, the bulk of our programming consisted of giving the Counselling Center, the Office of Services for Individuals with Disabilities, Coo-op Education, and other similar groups an hour.

Our major changeover came this past fall when we offered with our Media Producer to help these shops put their presentations on line, where they could be viewed on demand. Our faculty development programming since has followed the unified and iterative model, but, of course, we have to follow the CTL's prime directive and offer what programming our provost desires. As a result, since the provost considers metacognition an important tool for student retention and success, we have been so focused the past two years.

This fall, as part of the Provost's Speaker Series, Saundra McGuire, author of *Teach Students How To Learn* (2015), provided workshops on metacognitive strategies for both students and faculty. On the faculty side, we had over half of the full-time faculty participate. In preparation for her coming, we scheduled two consecutive semesters of Professional Learning Communities (PLCs) devoted to metacognition. In addition, we developed the ninth book in our "It Works for Me" Series as *It Works for Me, Metacognitively* (2016), collecting effective metacognitive strategies from not only our home campus but all around the country. In addition, for our spring semester ten-part Teaching and Learning Innovation Series (TLI), we are facilitating two workshops on "Incorporating Metacognition into Your Classroom: Concepts and Strategies."

The remainder of the TLI Series stresses key pedagogical concepts, such as critical reading, intuition in the classroom, quality matters and teaching online, using SSPS (a research program)for teaching and research, what great teachers do, planning and designing visual syllabi, what I learned at the SXSWedu (South by Southwest) conference, and how to use virtual labs in science classes. While all these topics do indeed center around pedagogy, even that focus does not seem tight enough.

Future Programming

We think that in the future we will have to stress some specific aspect or aspects (i.e., threads) of pedagogy. We came close with our thread of metacognition, but we would like to be more narrow next year. In fact, we are in the process of finishing a book for New Forums on *Transforming Your Students into Deep Learners* (2016), so our tentative plans suggest we will indeed structure programming around the major thread of deep learning.

7. 3 Principles for Innovating the Faculty Development Experience

(Posted 4 August 2015)

http://newforums.com/?s=3+Principles+for+Innovating+the+Faculty+Development+Experience

Since it's that time of year when New Faculty Orientation is almost upon us, we're once again excited and renewed about the opportunity. Yet, a little over a decade ago when we took over new faculty development at our university, we didn't like the plate we were served. All new tenure-track hires were put through a solid Monday-through-Friday week of activities that began at eight in the morning and lasted until five. Four days of sitting still in administrator-as-talking head information sessions were broken up one day by a five-hour bus ride, only occasionally with air conditioning and roller-coasting through the hills of eastern Kentucky. Mostly, new faculty were herded through HR, payroll, IT, benefits, ID picture-taking, parking, etc. with the result that by Friday afternoon their minds had been numbed by information overload, and the University had spent nearly $10,000 in the process.

Did you notice in this never-ending parade of indoctrination and torpor what key elements of a college professor duties weren't even mentioned?

Of course, we weren't immediately given the reins of this white elephant. As is the academic way, we had to get ourselves put on the New Faculty Orientation Committee (NFOC), then sit through endless hours of meetings dominated by administrators, PowerPoints, and tittering (higher education's equivalent of laughter). Gradually, by volunteering to look into problems or put together part of the week, we were ceded some power. And each year we moved up the hierarchal ladder toward control. Eventually, various members on the NFOC decided they had performed sufficient university service, retired, or took another job, and, of course, we expressed a willingness to take over leadership.

One of the first things we did was to look at a few years' surveys of what new faculty members were telling us about their week-long experiences. Then, studying the obstacles to overcome, we identified our strengths and brainstormed various meta-principles for innovation in the experience of new faculty. In so doing we derived four sweeping ideas for change.

Simplification

As former professors of English, we had often taught Henry David Thoreau's classic. In fact, his retreat to *Walden* (1854) was an experiment designed to confront life in order to distill it to its basic necessities, and because "Our life is frittered away by detail," his motto became "Simplify, simplify." Later, we came across *Learning To Think Things Through* (2000), wherein Gerry Nosich advocates reducing complicated things (e.g., college courses) to their "fundamental and powerful concepts" in order to help students learn them deeply.

Applying that principle to New Faculty Orientation, we decided to make two major changes right away to the traditional week-long program; after all, as long-time faculty members, we were very aware how much value professors place on time. First, we cut the number of days down from five to three, and then we lopped off the afternoons. Research had taught us that faculty more and more were viewing the profession as a nine-to-five job and that they were part of a generation raising millennial students—i.e., helicopter parents. Let's give them time, we reasoned, to take their kids to some morning activity—usually school—and be there when it ended.

Focus

In a previous post we pointed out that your unit's focus/goal must be what your boss says it is. What do you do, though, when you aren't given much direction? At most institutions, whether the goal is expressed or not, administrators are very happy to save money. One byproduct of simplification was that three days cost the University less than five, and eliminating a costly bus trip made financial dollars and cents.

Remember our description of New Faculty Orientation? What did you find missing? Our university's historic mission was teaching (yes, it was once a teachers' college), yet in the five days of indoctrination, not one word was said about teaching. We coined the motto EXCELLENCE IN TEACHING IS JOB ONE, made posters to that effect, and started signing our email with the phrase. We decided to devote one third of our week to teaching, and to stress its importance, we would lead with it. Day One became Pedagogy Day. In a later post we'll describe how this day works.

Atmosphere

In our first attempt at our new three-day approach to new faculty orientation, we still had two-days with a host of administrators greeting faculty and telling them what was expected of them. Most importantly, we realized that even though many had once been faculty, they had gone over to a dark side, where the preferred method of instruction was the PowerPoint lecture (to be fair, that approach was probably the preferred pedagogy when they joined the dark side).

We decided that even these administrator-heavy days had to be fun and interactive. Furthermore, that which was basically pure background information (e.g., the history of the University, how the counselling center works) could be presented in other forms such as email or even a large three-ring binder. Topics that demanded greater treatment became part of our fall roundtables (e.g., dealing with distressed students, the disabilities office, veterans affairs)—essentially a series of one-hour workshops.

These three meta-principles have served us well and have been melded into our unit's motto—"Helping teachers help students learn deeply."

8. The Future of Faculty Development: A Techtonic Shift

(Posted 7 October 2014)

http://newforums.com/future-faculty-development-techtonic-shift/

In "Preparing New Faculty for Leadership: Understanding and Addressing Needs (*To Improve the Academy* 33.1, September 2014, 57-73), Kelsch and Hawthorne point out how little new faculty "felt they knew about higher education beyond their discipline" (60). Sorcinelli et al suggest another reason faculty need professional development: they "will need to learn new skills or expand into new areas—new approaches to teaching, new ways to engage with communities, and new strategies or collaborations to pursue their research" (*Creating the Future of Faculty Development: Learning from the past, Understanding the Present*, 2006, 167). In our *Teaching Applied Creative Thinking* (2013) we suggest a new model for professorial responsibilities that includes mandatory faculty development (146-147). While we believe all these insights and ideas have merit, we'd like to suggest a new delivery system.

Our rationale for this system is based on changing demographics. At our institution we just finished a week of New Faculty Orientation (NFO), and the 62 members of the so-called Class of 2014 represent approximately 10% of the full-time faculty at Eastern Kentucky University. Cumulatively, half of the faculty at our school has turned over in the past five years. Both here and in the national literature we have noticed some trends concerning the higher educators of the 21st century:

- **Newer faculty view their profession as a 9:00-5:00 job**. As a result, one change we made in our NFO was starting at 9:00 and finishing by 1:00, creating a family-friendly atmosphere wherein the professors who are also parents (the helicopter phenomenon) can even take their kids to school and pick them up.
- As part of the Millennial Generation, **newer faculty are very tech savvy**. No doubt the highlight of NFO was not "graduation," but being given their own laptop (or seeing their comments instantly light up our "Tweet Board").
- **Newer faculty want what they want now**. In the non-academic arenas of their lives, newer faculty are used to grabbing their cellphone to make that important call or looking up a needed piece of information instantly on the Internet.

As a result, while we surrender to traditional faculty development for the new faculty's introduction to our university, and we continue to provide the familiar staples of workshops (e.g., Dee Fink on creating significant learning experiences), lunch-and-learns (e.g., a presentation on the University's academic integrity policy), and professional learning communities (e.g., gatherings of 5% of the school's faculty to implement flipping the classroom), we are this year experimenting with new technological forms of faculty development. Admittedly, part of our decision is based on low attendance at the traditional events.

First, we created an online course called "Achieving Excellence in Teaching" that we placed in each new faculty member's BlackBoard account. If the name of the course sounds familiar, it's because we adapted the course from our book *Achieving Excellence in Teaching* (2014). The course revolves around a fundamental and powerful concept, the top ten tips for terrific teaching, and runs the gamut from needed dispositions, to organization, to basic technical competence. The course takes approximately one hour to complete, provides a review and quiz at the end, and even offers successful accomplishers a certificate **whenever they need/want the training**.

Second, to further appeal to this tech audience, we are in the midst of creating a sort of academic Comcast system on our website www.tlc.eku.edu we call the **TEACHER'S TOOLBOX**. When it's complete, this PD on Demand platform will offer our busy, tech-savvy faculty the training in fundamental and powerful concepts for them to develop **whenever they need/want the training**.

Our first podcast, the one we consider most important, is based on the demographics of the typical EKU student as well as the character traits of the millennial student. One of the most fundamental and powerful concepts in writing, oral communication, and teaching is KNOW THY AUDIENCE, certainly the principle factor behind our techtonic shift, so we thought it best to begin with such a summary of the student population. How we present this information—i.e., the format of the podcast—we think is the key to a successful product.

And in a future post we'll analyze what we consider the essential traits of an effective podcast.

9. Is There Really a Teaching Revival Happening Now?

(Posted 20 July 2016)

http://newforums.com/is-there-really-a-teaching-revival-happening-now/

In *Academically Adrift* (2011), Richard Arum and Josipa Roksa present compelling evidence about the failure of American colleges and universities. "How much are students actually learning in contemporary higher education?" they ask. "The answer for many undergraduates, we have concluded, is not much" (34). In examining the development of critical thinking, complex reasoning, and writing skills, Arum and Roksa find that "An astounding proportion of students are progressing through higher education today without any measurable gains in general skills as assessed by the CLA [College Learning Assessment]" (36). While much of the blame for such a shoddy performance is placed on the shoulders of students for their lack of direction, poor study habits, and even academic fraud (14), faculty are also indicted for such things as:

- Lowering academic standards and raising course marks (7)
- Limited preparation, teaching, and advising time—i.e., 11 hours/week average (8)
- Lack of pedagogical training.

Reacting to this lack of learning in a recent article in *The Chronicle of Higher Education*, "Teaching Revival: Fresh Attention to the Classroom May Actually Stick this Time" (13 March 2015), Dan Berrett asserts that colleges are indeed turning their attention to pedagogy: "The quality of college teaching has been a concern for years. Change may finally be arriving, thanks to shifting student demographics, debates about the value of a degree, discoveries in the science of learning, and the influence of new technology" (B35). Unfortunately, as evidence Berrett cites improvements only at some major universities such as Harvard, the University of Michigan, and Columbia. What's interesting is the comparison of Arum and Roksa's use of multiple sources and wide-spread testing to expose the problem verses Berrett's minimalist citing of basically three institutions as a solution.

We would love to believe that suddenly faculty have become aware of their need for professional development, especially in pedagogical skills, but we don't see the evidence. What is most needed now is an Arum and Roksa-size survey of not only faculty but also of advanced-degree institutions. How much training, for instance, do aspiring physics Ph.D.s receive in what current evidence says are the best practices in teaching? Are candidates for Ph.D.s in English learning as much about assessment as Aristotle's *Poetics*?

Another good idea whose time has come is the expansion of the typical tripartite listing of faculty responsibilities of teaching, scholarship, and service to become a quartet. As we suggested in *Teaching Applied Creative Thinking* (2013), professional development needs to be added. How does the academy make such a monumental change?

Even professional development needs to be redefined. Too often, PD is conceived of as merely staying current in one's discipline. That definition seems a half-truth to us. Faculty need to upgrade their understanding of what brain science is telling us about teaching and learning as well as advances in technology. In the Commonwealth, the governing body, the Council on Postsecondary Education (CPE), has developed a faculty workgroup to coordinate such professional development in the state, and each May we put on a convention. Interested parties need only to Google Kentucky Pedagogicon 2015 to see the opportunities available, and we'd love to have you attend on 22 May 2015.

How many universities have created professional development plans for each faculty member? At some institutions such plans are as important as promotion and tenure (P&T). Some schools even write professional development plans into their P&T documents. At the very least, every faculty member should fill out such a document annually with his or her chair.

Will our academically adrift students be rescued? The expansion of professional development is just one of the possible lifelines. Ultimately, if faculty don't develop a disposition for what education researcher George Kuh calls "positive restlessness" or a desire to continually improve (Berrett, B37), our students may be beyond saving.

ESTABLISHING A CENTER OF TEACHING AND LEARNING (CTL)

By Charlie Sweet, Hal Blythe & Russell Carpenter

1. Why Centers of Teaching and Learning Have Advisory Boards

(Posted 17 September 2015)

http://newforums.com/why-centers-teaching-and-learning-have-advisory-boards/

In *Creating the Future of Faculty Development* (2006), Sorcinelli et al posit that faculty development has "entered a new age—the Age of the Network. Faculty, developers, and institutions alike are facing heightened expectations, and meeting these expectations will require a collaborative effort among all stakeholders in higher education" (pp. 4-5). New faculty developers need to recognize the importance of this observation as they go about building a center of teaching and learning (CTL). One area in which the Age of the Network comes up is with advisory boards.

Does your CTL have an advisory board? If it does, you might start to think about why the board exists; if it doesn't have one, you might consider adding one. If nothing else, advisory boards create a sense of ownership, of shared governance, and of a cross-stitching of campus constituents. Traditionally, advisory boards serve two purposes. They function as a two-way highway for CTLs—sometimes the information comes in and sometimes it goes out. Effective CTLs make use of both functions.

Input

When we began, we thought an advisory board was a necessity. While we knew we had to follow rule number one and do what our boss told us, we knew that we also had to address the needs of our constituents—faculty, departments, deans, and we would include our provost. In one sense it didn't matter what national trends told us what CTLs were doing, what we had to do was to respond to the immediate and specific needs of our folks. If the University developed a Quality Enhancement Program centering on creative thinking, it was up to us to offer programming—workshops, professional learning communities, and informational sessions—in support. If the faculty senate were taking up a new policy, we could do research for them on the area using our graduate assistant. If the Chairs Association asked us to tackle an area (e.g., the Scholarship of Teaching and Learning), we did.

One different avenue of aid we established early was the book. If the University had a problem area, we wrote a book on it. Back a few years ago, for example, the University was trying to define the relationship between a professor's traditional duties of scholarship and instruction. We ended up doing two collections through New Forums on the topic, *It Works For Me as a Scholar Teacher* (2008) and *It Works For Me: Becoming a Publishing Scholar/Researcher* (2010). Of course, technology has advanced since then; were we aiming at the same goal now, we might create an e-book, open our own You Tube channel, or develop an electronic repository for the materials.

Output

Advisory Boards also serve to disseminate information. In the beginning when we needed publicity, we had our board members deliver the information to their constituents. Again, over the years technology has changed many things. We now have our own website to advertise professional development opportunities, and we can even target various groups on campus (e.g., new faculty). We can use the University's daily information e-system, and Rusty's Social Media Committee has become quite proficient at tweeting key events before, during, and after. As we now speak regularly with the provost and president, we can usually persuade their offices to disperse any information.

The Future—To Board or Not To Board?

At this point a good question might be: has technological progress replaced the need for advisory boards? Even if we believed the answer was yes, we would till argue for employing advisory boards because of the notion of shared governance, and that impression is one worth creating at first. Also, you have the option to convene Advisory Boards when you need to solve problems, for issues that warrant face-to-face communication. Down the road you may find less need to convene the advisory board as often, but keeping the board works for another important reason—expertise. Not everyone on your board has the same basic interests and backgrounds. For example, at a meeting this morning of the board, we discovered that one of the members was quite proficient at assessment and was very willing to help us draw up an instrument to evaluate our professional learning communities. Another member suddenly displayed a background in pedagogical software. We'll bet at future meetings we continue to discover our members have other amazing knowledge and talent.

One final point. Having done the research on brainstorming, and having the experience of facilitating many campus committees, organizations, and work groups, we're great believers in small groups—say, no larger than seven—accomplishing more. With seven members you have time for everyone's input, and you will have all the input you need.

Tips For Implementation

A. In determining whether to have a board, <u>start not with your own preference but with that of the person to whom you report.</u>

B. If that person believes in a board, <u>come to a consensus of what type of board is desired</u>. Sometimes your boss will insist that person X be or not be on the board.

C. <u>Pick your battles</u>. The longer you have been in business, the greater your CTL's success, and the better your relationship with your superior, the better your chances of doing things your way.

D. <u>Always try to place one person on the board you can count on and one person with whom you often find yourself disagreeing.</u> You need support, but you also need different perspectives. Neither all yes people nor all no people will lead to an effective CTL.

Discussion Questions

A. The chapter posits two central purposes for the advisory board, input and output. Are there other valid reasons for an Advisory Board? Is the figurehead position a reason itself—i.e., having a board so that you can say you have a board?

B. At its conclusion the chapter suggests that small boards ("no larger than seven") function best. What do you think is the optimal size of a board? Are boards actually political tools creating the illusion of participation? Should CTLs find the best people on campus or the best political mix?

Activities

A. Assuming your CTL does not have an advisory board, draw up a list for both types—the best people and the best political mix. Ask yourself which board would you prefer in reality. Does a third possibility emerge, an amalgam of the two previous types?

B. Assuming your CTL has a board, create a chart in which in column one you list the members and columns two and three are labelled "Best People" and "Best Political Mix." Where do your board members fit?

Section References

Mooney, K. (2010). Working with a faculty development committee. In K. Gillespie and D. Robertson (Eds.), *A guide to faculty development* (pp. 53-66). San Francisco: Jossey-Bass.

2. What Services Should a Center of Teaching and Learning Offer?

(Posted 23 September 2015)

http://newforums.com/what-services-should-a-center-of-teaching-and-learning-offer/

According to a 2005 survey by Sorcinelli et al as reported in *Creating the Future of Faculty Development* (2006), respondents identified eight key issues for CTLs:

- Teaching for student-centered learning
- New faculty development
- Integrating technology into traditional teaching and learning settings
- Active, inquiry-based, or problem-based learning
- Assessment of student learning outcomes
- Multiculturalism and diversity related to teaching
- Scholarship of Teaching
- Writing Across the Curriculum (p. 72).

In *A Guide to Faculty Development* (2010), Virginia Lee compiles a list of ten programs/services that can most impact an institution:
- Workshops
- Individual consultations
- Classroom observations
- Orientations
- Grants
- Faculty fellows
- Teaching circles
- Faculty learning communities
- Management of grant-funded projects
- Engagement in national projects (pp. 26-28).

So the question becomes, what programs and services should your CTL provide for your campus?

Review And Advice

In previous posts we have stressed two major factors in determining what to offer:
- What does your boss want?
- What does your advisory board want?

And now we'd like to suggest a third component. **What would you like to do**? More specifically, given your institution's funding of you, the space offered, the support given, and even your allotted time, **what are you capable of doing**? Our friend and one-time director of a CTL at the University of Oklahoma, Dee Fink, did a presentation here last year and recommended that every CTL be funded at ½ to 1% of faculty salaries and benefits of the group it is being asked to serve. In reality, we doubt many CTLs receive this much University "grace," so as director, your job comes down to balancing the support realities, your boss's desire, and your board's advice. Our advice is two-part.

One, favor your boss' wishes.

Two, most schools have adopted as their unofficial motto today "Do more with less." We advise the minimalist approach. It is better, especially when starting out, to do a few programs well than to do a lot of programs in mediocre fashion. As you become successful, you can then argue for more support to increase your programming. Similarly, if you think you are trying to do too much, consider cutting back.

Actual Programming

The program that we believe offers the potential for success and saturation is **orientation**. In previous posts we have talked about how we offer orientation programs to four groups:
- New tenure-track Faculty (approximately 50/year)

- Part-time Faculty (approximately 75/year)
- University Orientation Faculty (approximately 60/year)
- Graduate Teaching Assistants (approximately 40/year).

Over the past ten years we have discovered that our usual workshops/roundtables draw over an academic year about 10% of the faculty. We're not positive of the national average, but we know from sitting on the state's faculty development workgroup that our figure is consistent with other institutions of higher learning in the commonwealth. Our university has approximately 600 full-time instructors, so while we may reach only 50 each year through orientation, we reach 50 new individuals each year. In addition, we have the participation of the other teaching groups. If you wish to effect a culture shift on your campus as we did with our EXCELLENCE IN TEACHING IS JOB ONE initiative, orientation is a good priority.

A second offering that satisfies bosses, boards, and faculty is **informational roundtables**. When we started, our boss thought it important that we offer a fall series of roundtables for new faculty, highlighting basic informational services—i.e., campus services of which faculty need to be aware. Thus, once a week every fall we have presentations on the University's academic integrity program, Co-op, opportunities in teaching abroad, mentoring student scholars, counselling center, the 911 program, accommodating students with disabilities, and even grants. All of these programs present key information faculty must know—e.g., pregnancy is now part of Title IX, attendance must be taken, crimes must be reported. What the faculty don't know can hurt them and, more importantly, their employer. What we are doing is converting all these presentations to podcasts, but that's the subject of another post.

A third offering is **workshops**, some which we do every fall and others that we rotate through or add in. For instance, this fall we are providing workshops in a new journal of undergraduate research, emerging technologies, teaching effective design and creativity, the IDEA form (offered every fall because the University has chosen to use this assessment instrument), making polished videos, teaching with social media, best practices in classroom observation, and working smarter through the Scholarship of Teaching and Learning (SOTL).

A fourth key service deals with consultation and classroom observation, but that, too, is a post for next time.

Tips For Implementation

A. After talking with your superior about what services s/he thinks should be prioritized, <u>utilize your Institutional Research unit to create a campus-wide survey</u> of what services both administrators and faculty think you should offer. Be sure to code the survey so that you can tell faculty preferences from administrative desires. You will need support from both groups to succeed.

B. <u>Build a network</u>. Make friends with people in power across campus. Go to lunch with more than just the same old people. Show up at events put on by campus organizations with which you might be able to collaborate. Send out congratulatory emails to faculty and administrators for individual accomplishments—awards, publications, and presentations.

C. <u>Take a realistic approach</u>. While the faculty might desire monthly appearances of Dee Fink, administrators will explain the money does not exist for such extravagance.

D. <u>Beware of offering free gifts</u>. If you provide stipends in the beginning for every professional learning community, faculty will sign up, but come to expect such stipends for every PLC. If you offer a few door prizes at events, faculty will become upset because more people will not receive free stuff than those who will.

Discussion Questions

A. What steps can you take to build an effective network? Have you considered, for instance, collaborating with the head of Institutional Research on an article that reaches across your domains? Have you worked with any campus units on projects, such as creation of a discipline-specific journal or a summer camp for STEM students?

B. How do you best weave your unit into the basic fabric of the university? How high up the food chain do you report? Are you mentioned in the latest iteration of the university's strategic plan?

C. How do you let people know about your services? Do you have a website? Do you send out mass notices to the faculty? Do you use flyers? Do you visit individual colleges and departments to trumpet your services? Do you enlarge your presence by connecting to statewide, regional, and national faculty development organizations?

Activities

A. If your CTL is small (and many are), create a list that prioritizes the three major services you would like to provide. Now run a reality check. Do you have the support and funding to pull it off?

B. Does your university offer a new faculty orientation? If not, offer to create one for both fulltime and part-time professors. If it exists somewhere else, get yourself on that advisory board. The unit that controls new faculty orientation has an excellent chance of shaping campus culture.

Section References

- Sorcinelli, M., Austin, A., Eddy, P., & Beach, A. (2010). *Creating the future of faculty development: Learning from the past, understanding the present.* Bolton, MA: Anker.

3. Types and Characteristics of Successful Faculty Programming

(Posted 11 November 2015)

http://newforums.com/types-characteristics-successful-faculty-programming/

So now that you have a CTL to run, you're going to have to decide what kind of programming to put on. As mentioned earlier, your boss has given you some input and so has your advisory board, but there's one more step you could take. When we took over this CTL, we got together with Institutional Research to create a survey, which we emailed to the entire faculty. What we desired to know was what kind of programming the faculty needed and wanted. In our case, the majority of answers centered on recent technology and help with scholarship.

Programming can be complex because CTLs usually serve varying audiences. Think of the possibilities:
- New full-time faculty
- New adjunct faculty
- Full-time faculty
- Others: Teachings Assistants, Specialized Class Instructors, Administrators.

As a result, CTLs must plan the programming to serve all groups. Some of the programs will overlap, but all will not.

Informative Sessions

For us, since our bosses and advisory board prioritize new faculty orientation, we offer fall programming that introduces this cohort to important services on campus that we didn't have time to explore during new faculty orientation. Most of these topics are things faculty members really need to know in order to be successful, and the programming also serves to emphasize that fact.

For instance, we began this fall's programming on the third day of the semester with a session on the University's academic integrity policy, moderated by a lawyer from that office. Faculty members can encounter cheating from day one, so it's important to begin with this offering.

Our second presentation is not so time sensitive nor would the knowledge of its contents be mandatory. We have a representative from the University's co-op and career services office discuss what they can do to help students. Faculty are encouraged to make sure their students also receive this information as co-op is often a great first step toward a permanent job. We offer our next session on teaching abroad opportunities. For faculty on nine-month contracts, this program offers not only summer employment, but a chance to go overseas. During the semester we also provide informative sessions by the Office of Undergraduate

Research and Creative Endeavors, University-funded scholarship and grant opportunities, accommodating students with disabilities, dealing with distressed students, administering the IDEA (a mandatory campus-wide evaluation of teaching).

Workshops

Complementing these "things it would help you to know" sessions are our workshops, and we try to offer at least one a month. With our advisory board and with occasional input from the Faculty Senate and the Chairs Association, we pick from a combination of needed and hot topics. This fall, for instances, we are holding sessions on the following topics:
- Contributing to the new *Kentucky Journal of Undergraduate Research*
- Beyond Brainstorming: Teaching Effective Design and Creativity
- Making Simple, Polished Videos for Your Classroom
- Teaching and Learning with Social Media
- Best Practices for Peer Observation of Teaching, and
- Working Smarter Through SOTL.

Workshops last longer than purely informative sessions—usually one and one-half to three hours and contain more interactive materials. Participants may learn about editing videos, the best way to have a peer observe your teaching, how to tie a SOTL research project to your teaching, or even how various social media forms can be incorporated into your teaching. While the informational sessions rarely change, new workshops are added each semester.

Administrative-Sponsored Events

Through trial and error, we've found another type of event—administration-sponsored ones. What got us started was talking with a vice-president for student affairs who wanted a forum to discuss the typical EKU student. For instance, because the last three University presidents and four provosts want to build a rapport with the faculty, we have hosted what we call Fireside Chats. Basically, any administrator sits in from of our meeting room's fireplace and runs a type of press conference. Our current president so likes the Fireside Chat concept that he is running six this semester.

Characteristics of Good Programs

Over the years we've figured out a few guiding principles for successful programming:
- <u>Respond to the desires</u> of faculty and administrators.
- <u>Keep it current</u>. Schedule sessions that provide unique perspectives on current topics or new takes on traditional topics. Faculty members want to know that what they're hearing is the latest and greatest.
- <u>Connect</u>. Help faculty connect sessions with others on related or complementary top-

ics. Sessions can build on one another to provide a more cohesive experience for new and returning faculty.
- <u>Provide food</u> ("If you feed them, they will come"). Our Fireside Chats normally occur around 8:30 so we offer a healthy continental breakfast with as much coffee as they can drink. Other sessions start at 11:00 or 11:15 (depending on the class pattern) so we set up a lunch table.
- <u>Advertise</u>. New faculty receive a notebook with all of this information as well as personalized email for each session. The sessions are also listed on our website, and notice is made eight days out and one day out on the campus email system.
- <u>Follow up each session with an electronic evaluation</u> (more on this another time). Workshop evaluations ask about application to the faculty member's course.
- <u>Make participants sign in</u> and supply their email address. This information is crucial for assessment, and the federal government requires records on food distribution.
- <u>Develop interactive sessions</u>. All event presenters are provided with a list of tips that range from how to structure a PowerPoint to how to be maximally interactive.
- <u>Work on making all events part of a for-credit program</u> (e.g., certificate). This concept is another we will expand on later.

Tips For Implementation

A. <u>Determine your focus</u>. In the beginning we provided roundtables that were 80% service-oriented—i.e., we had various groups such as Study Abroad and Cooperative Education present, but this year we switched our focus from service to faculty development in pedagogy, technology, and scholarship. In the beginning our roundtables were aimed primarily at new faculty. Now the focus is on the faculty at large.

B. <u>Review</u> "Characteristics of Good Programs" in the Overview.

Discussion Questions

A. If you decide to perform a needs assessment, what would be the most efficient way to survey the faculty (both full-time and part-time), professional staff, and administrators?

B. Given your CTL's budget, what types of programming are possible? How many events could you offer per semester given the cost of materials, food, etc.?

C. How could you go about securing presenters and facilitators for your events? Should you choose to offer incentives to these individuals? If so, could you afford stipends or other incentives given your CTL's budget and administrative attitudes?

D. How could you best assess the value of programming? Should you try for longitudinal tracking of the effects of programming on participants? If so, how could you implement the process?

E. Should you consider linking semester or year-long programming through a theme?

Activities

A. Form a focus group drawn from a diversity of faculty, professional staff, and administrators and allow them to discuss what they believe to be the most significant current "needs" on campus.

B. Contact your counterparts on benchmark campuses, and query them on what the most successful programs have been in recent semesters. Ask about those programs that have lacked popularity or positive effect. Ask for your counterparts' ideas on reasons for these successes and failures.

Section References

Sorcinelli, M., Austin, A., Eddy, P., & Beach, A. (2006). *Creating the future of faculty development: Learning from the past, understanding the present.* Bolton, MA: Anker.

4. 14 Guidelines for Successful Higher Ed Faculty Workshops

(Posted 2 March 2016)

http://newforums.com/14-guidelines-successful-higher-ed-faculty-workshops/

One question that comes up quite often with our oversight of all things under our auspices is: how involved should we as the Executive Committee be over presentations and workshops that occur under our general center for teaching & learning (CTL) banner or that specifically of the Faculty Innovators? One school of thought says treat them like your children who have to be given a certain amount of latitude to even fail, while another point of view claims that any event labelled as coming from us reflects upon us, and if it looks bad, we look bad.

As we evolve our programs, we try to offer more and more guidance to those who in essence represent us. While the Faculty Innovators receive more basic training in everything from conducting workshops to consulting with faculty clients, we provide even volunteers with some basic presentation guidelines that are a living document. Every time we observe a workshop, we seem to add to or tweak our document.

Here are some fundamental guidelines:

1. In your presentation, no matter your content the main thing you should hope to accomplish is to be an effective model for good teaching. Everything you do should reflect a pedagogical best practice.

2. In that vein, plan for an interactive workshop, not a PowerPoint-supported lecture.

3. Any instructions, directions, or even presentation of fundamental and powerful concepts should take no more than five minutes.

4. Utilize two to three exercises that your audience can undertake. You can employ reflection, pair-and-share, or even larger group work. An alternative might be to utilize a single case study that covers your major points.

5. Whatever exercises your audience performs, be sure to plan for a report-out and reaction (by you and the other participants) to whatever is reported. Your audience must be made to believe that their input matters.

6. Where appropriate, intentionally utilize Bloom's Taxonomy, and make your audience understand not only that you are using it, but why.

7. Structure your presentation around the basic classroom organizational pattern of **C.R.I.S.P.**:

- **C**ontextualize: at the beginning make sure your audience is provided with the fundamental and powerful concepts (FPCs) you intend to cover. Clearly outline your Faculty Learning Objectives (FLOs) for the session. Demonstrate quickly why these FPCs are important to the audience.
- **R**eview: tie your subject to materials previously covered in earlier sessions or that are University themes. We, for instance, use the aegis of the Teaching & Learning Innovations Series (TLI), and we often tie to our basic campus milestones (e.g., New Faculty Orientation, the Provost's Speaker Series, Scholarship Week, the Pedagogicon). The key notion here is that new knowledge is built on old.
- **I**terate: make certain your fundamental and powerful concepts come up a few times and in different ways (e.g., PowerPoint, pair-and-share, or even Q & A).
- **S**ummarize: Make certain you stop your workshop five minutes before the allotted time period ends so that you can simplify, synthesize, and strategize.
- **P**review: if possible, know what event comes next in the series so that you can tie it to what you have done.

8. As with your own classes, arrive early and stay afterwards. Use the time to build rapport, answer questions, and even plant intellectual seeds.

9. Make the workshop entertaining. Be interesting and humorous. While some educational jargon is unavoidable, balance it with cultural and pop cultural allusions.

10. Use the Mentor from the Middle methodology. Rather than stay at the front of the class, mingle with your audience whether you are providing information or helping them with their exercises.

11. Communicate effectively. Speak clearly and slowly. Make eye contact. Show everyone your face. If you know some of your colleagues in the audience, use their names.

12. Make sure you provide a survey for your participants. CTLs should develop such an evaluation rubric as well as a methodology for transmitting it to your audience (e.g., hand out or send electronically).

13. Offer handouts during the session and when possible provide them electronically to participants. CTLs should develop repositories where such documents can be easily located.

14. Finally, the best workshops do not try to cover a broad area, but focus on a single,

important aspect of a larger concern. They center on a fundamental and powerful concept that can be presented by a facilitator and applied by an audience.

References

Sweet, C. & Blythe, H. (2008). Keeping your classroom C.R.I.S.P. *NEA Higher Education Advocate, 26*(2), 5-8.

Tips For Implementation

A. As with all CTL programming, survey faculty (both full-time and part-time), professional staff, and administrators to determine current campus needs.

B. Distill the broad list of needs to those focused fundamental and powerful concepts that will most benefit the greatest number of individuals across campus.

C. Identify those colleagues most qualified to conduct workshops on these areas, and contact them to determine their desire/willingness to facilitate as well as their availability.

D. Develop a set of guidelines for facilitators to ensure that each workshop runs smoothly and achieves optimal results.

E. Create an assessment instrument that will gauge both the participant's satisfaction and willingness/plans to employ strategies presented in the workshops.

Discussion Questions

A. Does your CTL have appropriate spaces for conducting workshops? Are these spaces equipped with the necessary equipment—tables, flipcharts, whiteboards, wifi access, etc.?

B. Do you have an effective protocol for identifying and securing workshop facilitators, advertising the workshops and enrolling participants, supplying needed ancillaries, and assessing sessions?

C. Have you thought about your overall goals for the workshops? Do you see them as individual units or as parts of your overall programming? Have you considered linking the workshops through a theme?

D. Have you considered developing a set of guidelines for workshop presenters? How rigid should these guidelines be? How would you enforce these guidelines?

Activities

A. Draft a set of guidelines for workshop facilitators. Consider such aspects as length, focus, methodology, use of technology, and presentation strategies.

B. Create a user-friendly assessment tool to gauge participants' satisfaction with the workshop and willingness to employ in their classroom one or more of the strategies presented.

Section References

Sorcinelli, M., Austin, A., Eddy, P. & Beach, A. (2006). *Creating the future of faculty development: Learning from the past, understanding the present.* Bolton, MA: Anker.

5. To Belong or Not Belong to POD in Higher Education?

(Posted 8 June 2016)

http://newforums.com/to-belong-or-not-belong-to-pod-in-higher-education/

We may be one of the few centers for teaching and learning (CTLs) that do not belong to POD (the Professional and Organizational Development Network in Higher Education), a professional organization that Sorcinelli reported in 2006 contained 1400 members. We used to belong, but their institutional fee was too large of an item to maintain on our budget, a budget which we think could be among the lowest in the nation. We also confess that we have never been to POD's annual conference.

Should we belong? Probably. The benefits of being able to reach out to other CTLs for solutions to common problems are great. But despite not subscribing to a national service, we are not totally alone.

State Organization

Luckily, our state has its own mini-POD. All higher education in the commonwealth is governed by the Council on Postsecondary Education (CPE), which years ago created the CPE Faculty Development Workgroup (FDW). Consisting of the six regional comprehensive universities, the University of Kentucky, the University of Louisville, 19 independent schools, and the state's community college system, this group has its own bylaws, a rotating annual facilitator, four meetings per year (half accomplished online), and a yearly conference.

As members of the FDW, we have primarily contributed to the group's well-being throughout the past decade. In fact, in six of the last ten years, we have been in charge of the group's conference. Three years ago we moved it to our university and renamed it the Kentucky Pedagogicon and then just The Pedagogicon (usually followed by its year).

What probably prodded us into this post was that last Friday we held Pedagogicon 2016, and the entire conference experience has weighed heavily on our minds. After a few years of increased attendance, this year the number of conferees fell off. Ironically, as we have added attendees from Massachusetts, Texas, and even Toronto, three of our major regionals did not send a single person to the conference, nor did they actually name a representative to our group.

And that decline we directly attribute to the gradual disintegration of the FDW. In point of fact, one of our counterparts at another state institution told us at the Pedagogicon that the CPE FDW has fallen to the bottom of her list of priorities. Indeed, this year the group met only once online, and we had to hold a working BBQ the night before the conference to get everyone up to date. Fittingly, only three persons attended, one of whom represented the CPE.

The principle is simple—a chain is only as strong as its weakest link.

So we sit here at the end of another academic year trying to figure out what direction to go. As we see it, we have three choices (or some combination thereof):

1) Drop out of the FDW (if we can).
2) Join POD.
3) Rejuvenate the FDW.

We have chosen option #3, and we may even find the money to join POD in the fall, especially since its national conference is being held this fall less than a hundred miles away.

Some Suggestions For Rebuilding

As we try to generate more interest in the state workgroup, we have come up with several suggestions for doing so.

1. <u>Survey the members</u>. At last week's Pedagogicon and the pre-conference BBQ, we talked with various college representatives as well as some from the CPE. All of those contacted offered some suggestions, but most were about the conference and not the FDW.

2. <u>Contact the provosts</u> at the member institutions that do not have a representative and ask if these administrators will select someone.

3. <u>Remind all that the higher ed accrediting agency</u> to which we belong, SACS, has SACSCOC Principles of Accreditation (2012) that include faculty development as a Comprehensive Standard: "3.7.3 The institution provides ongoing professional development of faculty as teachers, scholars, and practitioners." Obviously, the FDW and its Pedagogicon offers a partial way of fulfilling that requirement.

4. <u>Contact the state's CPE</u> to have them call together a meeting of the workgroup. Perhaps if we can get this authority to exert some influence, the group can be revitalized.

Final Thoughts

Sometimes we blame ourselves for the FDW's decline. The group's basic function for as long as we have belonged has been to provide a state-wide conference for the exchange of the best pedagogical strategies. Maybe by handling those duties ourselves for 60% of the decade, we have caused other state schools to feel less relevant and less participatory.

In any case, belonging to a larger group with similar concerns, be it the FDW or POD, seems absolutely necessary.

Tips For Implementation

A. Determine if your CTL or faculty development program can function effectively on its own or if association with a larger organization would be beneficial.

B. If you choose to join a large organization, do some ground work to determine which group or groups for which your program is most suited.

C. Contact the most suitable groups to find out about any membership requirements or costs.

D. Investigate publications by the group, and, if possible, attend one of their conferences.

Discussion Questions

A. How closely joined are the institutions, both public and private, in your state? Does a governing body exist?

B. Does your program have adequate funding to participate in a state, regional, or national organization?

C. How involved with a larger organization do you wish to become? Would you like to assume a leadership role in a larger organization?

Activities

A. Go online to research some possible organizations with which you might affiliate.

B. Contact your counterparts with programs that are members of prospective organizations and get their thoughts on the pros and cons of membership.

6. Is Your Center of Teaching and Learning a Hammer or Nail?

(Posted 27 July 2016)

http://newforums.com/is-your-center-of-teaching-and-learning-be-a-hammer-or-nail/

Years ago Paul Simon told us that "I'd rather be a hammer than a nail." In essence, every Center of Teaching and Learning (CTL) has to decide what it wants to be. Is it a traditional nail being hammered into shape, or is it a proactive force doing the shaping?

In a previous post, we emphasized that "The Faculty Developer's Most Important Question" is "to whom do you report" and the key to a CTL's activities is "what matters most is what matters most to your boss."

But the second most important question is: into what do you want to innovate your CTL? Yes, you have a mission, but that mission is general. Administrators, technologies, and even theories of faculty development will change over the years, but what you want to be able to do is to change at least with the tide or even better, ahead of it. In our way of thinking a CTL exists to provide pedagogical development to the faculty and has nearly nothing to do with disciplines such as chemistry staying current in their field. Sure, had we funding enough, we might want to co-sponsor a noted speaker in psychology or provide a venue for a campus-wide event, but a CTL's focus MUST be on pedagogy.

Appropriately, our CTL's mission is intentionally pedagogical in theory and practice: "Helping teachers help students learn deeply." And while we do exactly what our boss—actually we serve a provost and a dean—wants, we have adopted the hammer approach and try to nudge them in the direction our experience and research tell us to go.

So the question becomes how do you as director of your CTL know what direction to nudge them? Be deliberate—<u>make a list of all the things that you think you could accomplish as a CTL</u>. If you're not sure of the possibilities, check out other CTLs or even POD (Professional and Organizational Network in Higher Education) website. Then, given both your expertise and your unit's budget, prioritize the list. Start small. It's better to do a few things well and establish a good reputation than to create a mediocre unit that in its attempt to be all things does less and ruins your credibility.

Be ready for missteps. One of our original programs, for example, offered to send faculty to the famed Lilly Conference on College Teaching and Learning. What we encountered was a logistical nightmare in trying to get faculty to commit, to carpool, and arranging for their minute preferences (e.g., dietary). After a few years, we realized that our effort was eating up almost 50% of our budget and we had no way of knowing the program's effect on teaching and student learning. As a result, we modified the program into seven "Lillyships," wherein we supported only those faculty who appeared on the Lilly program.

Another problem developed when we assumed control of New Faculty Orientation. As the University draws primarily from a 22-county region (we are a regional university), traditionally new faculty were sent on a bus tour of the region. While the trip may have been good P.R. for the University, it wasn't helping our new faculty pedagogically, and it was costing us almost $3000. In fact, we inherited a New Faculty Orientation that had little to do with pedagogy (as we discussed in a previous post).

Back to our list. What did we convince our bosses we could do well? What would give them the biggest bang for the buck? Number one on our list was New Faculty Orientation. If the University were hiring between 50 and 60 new faculty per year—and academic churn is much greater now than when we arrived on campus—that meant every five years more than one-third of the faculty turned over. To effect a cultural change, it is much easier to start on the ground floor than with those who have settled in. In addition to new faculty, we also orient over 50 part-time faculty per year, almost 45 graduate teaching assistants, and the 60-plus cadre of instructors who teach the University's first-year orientation class.

Two hundred instructors mentored in best pedagogical practices would be enough if that were all we did.

Next time we'll discuss how we hammered out various other programs that reflected our primary pedagogical purpose.

Tips For Implementation

A. Determine, along with your "boss," the desired role of your program.

B. Determine your program's capacity in terms of personnel, space, resources, and funding.

C. Determine exactly how you think your time and resources can be used most effectively.

Discussion Questions

A. How deeply embedded in the campus fabric should a faculty development program be?

B. With what kind and how many roles do you feel comfortable?

Activities

A. Create a survey to determine what services outside your usual ones you might render to units on campus.

B. Check with counterparts at similar institutions to find out what services they render.

7. The X-Factor: One Result of Success

(Posted 30 March 2016)

http://newforums.com/the-x-factor-one-result-of-success/

"Success," suggested Emily Dickinson, "is counted sweetest by those who ne'er succeed." We'd like to add a corollary to the Belle of Amherst's famous pronouncement. SUCCESS IS COUNTED SWEETER BY THOSE WHO OFT EXCEED.

Simply put, success begets success. The more you accomplish as a center of teaching and learning (CTL), the more you will be asked to accomplish.

As we pointed out in an earlier blog, the most important function you have is pleasing your boss. If you don't, we know what happens, but if you do, your boss will come to you more often with tasks. When she started bringing in outside campus names to present workshops, we suggested she name her idea—hence, the Provost's Professional Development Speaker Series was born. When the Provost needed help with setting up workshops on alignment and assessment, we offered to help because we knew her chosen developer, Dee Fink. Those workshops were so successful that we brought Dee back for our New Faculty Orientation. And the next time the Provost needed help with advertising and establishing workshops for her series, she turned to us. Just last semester, we set up a workshop for which almost 50% of our full-time faculty participated.

Sometimes when you put on a workshop, someone in attendance thinks you could present a specialized workshop for his/her college, department, or program. We have been asked to do redo the workshop we did for new faculty on pedagogy for half of our College of Justice and Safety. Another time we established a similar workshop for the library's teaching staff at a summer retreat. Earlier this semester we held a successful workshop on metacognition that drew almost 10% of the faculty. Immediately, our retention team asked for us to explain to them how a student survey we developed on metacognition could aid student success. What we didn't know was that beside the 50+ administrators in attendance, our presentation was televised to all our regional campuses. When Housing saw our success with professional learning communities (PLCs), they asked us to show them how to run PLCs within the dorms.

Sometimes other superiors ask a favor. Because of our prolific output of writing, our dean has asked us to proofread various academic documents. One day the President of the University called us and said they had a mere six hours to write and submit an application to host a national vice-presidential debate. We took their draft, and in five hours the President had his document. That led to us having to rewrite a new brochure for the first year of the campus' new Arts Center (we did get some choice seating out of that one). Another time our Title IX coordinator, knowing we performed classroom observations of faculty instructors, asked us to observe her presentation and make some recommendations for improving it.

Sometimes when they have nowhere else to go, administrators come to us. When, for instance, the person who ran the Bachelor of Individualized Studies (BIS) program suddenly retired, the Provost at the time, having no place else to turn, asked us to administer the BIS. That was ten years ago, and the BIS is still part of our strategic plan even though our main charge is to work with faculty, not students. Ten years ago also, a group of faculty honored as Foundation Professors (a rank above full professor at our university) formed a group known as the Society of Foundation Professors (SFP), but they needed an attachment to some extant campus unit in order to be funded. "Home," Robert Frost famously asserted, "is the place where, when you have to go there, they have to take you in." If you were to guess where the SFP home has been since its inception, we're sure our Teaching& Learning Center came to mind. And because success grows on success, when the Advancement unit on campus wanted to start a giving campaign through the SFP, they asked us to help. As a result, we created the popular series "If It Weren't for Professor X . . ." for the Alumni Magazine, wherein alums were solicited to send in testimonies about their favorite professor and donations.

Along the way, since our university does not have one, we've become the unofficial ombudsperson. And when some group uses our space for a meeting and can't make their tech work, you'd probably think their first call was campus IT . . . and you'd be wrong.

Is all the extra work worth it? The good news is that builds great good will; the bad news is that the X-factor takes up a lot of time and energy. In the long run, though, our funding has increased, and our CTL is mentioned specifically in the University's new strategic plan.

And as Mae West once observed, "Too much of a good thing can be wonderful."

Tips For Implementation

A. Do a quick assessment of your services provided in relationship to the number and duties of the personnel in your shop. Do you have more duties than personnel available to cover them?

B. Are your personnel stretched so thin by their work that its quantity, quality, and attitude toward suffer?

C. Determine if it is best for you to take on more work and try to acquire new personnel.

Discussion Questions

1. The English poet-philosopher William Blake once claimed, "How can we know what is enough until we know what is more than enough." By the time we discover that the next added task is "more than enough," the camel's back is often broken. Are there ways to predetermine what saying "yes" (and even "no") means?

2. What are the measures for a success with a CTL? Do you have to win a Hesburg Award from POD? Is publishing a paper/book on a recent success sufficient reward? Is success only measured by the praise of the "boss" and perhaps a bonus/raise?

CREATING A FACULTY DEVELOPMENT PROGRAM

By Charlie Sweet, Hal Blythe & Russell Carpenter

A. Instituting Faculty Innovators and The Faculty Innovation Network

By Charlie Sweet, Hal Blythe & Russell Carpenter

1. Faculty Innovators: The Key to the Future of Faculty Development

(Posted 6 January 2016)

http://newforums.com/faculty-innovators-the-key-to-the-future-of-faculty-development/

Background

Anyone who has been in faculty development for a while knows its main problem: the very clientele CTLs (Centers for Teaching & Learning) are charged with developing do not attend the events put on for them. Here, we have tried different times of the day for presentations and workshops, different locations, bribes (food usually; books sometimes), various formats, assorted presenters, and even asking the provost to make some Professional Development (PD) mandatory, but nothing seems to gain traction for long.

Unfortunately, our CTL's experience is not isolated. Nationally, CTL programs seem stuck with about a 10% saturation rate—i.e., 90% of the faculty remain untouched by efforts to develop them professionally. The reasons given often revolve around increased faculty responsibilities and concomitant loss of time. The rise of technology has, among other things, created a cohort of online teachers who may never set foot on campus. Whatever the suggestions, the "if you build it, they will come" mentality has proven to be ineffective in dealing with the new realities of PD.

We have developed a couple of solutions to deal with the attendance problem that we'll be covering in the next few weeks. Simply put, we decided that if they won't come to us, we'll go to them, and the lynchpin of our grand idea is the **Faculty Innovator** (FI).

What Are Faculty Innovators?

The Faculty Innovator Program went from an idea to an implemented experiment in less than six months. We started putting the idea into practice long before the entire initiative was fleshed out and thus is an example of the applied creative thinking strategy we refer to as **nascent programming**. Nascent programming represents extreme risk-taking, of going with a beta program or prototype before all the kinks are worked out. Nascent programming assumes that the **risk** of failure is outweighed by the possibility of success, that the potential for doing something looms larger than not doing it, and that even in failing we gain valuable insights.

Our Faculty Innovator Program consists of a cadre of selected faculty members with expertise in teaching, learning strategies, classroom techniques, up-to-date technologies, and a strong desire to share that expertise with other faculty. In the spring of this year, a full six months before the start of the fall semester, we chose seven faculty members with at least one from each of the five colleges at our institution. Since then the Dean of Libraries has supported an eighth innovator, the online administration is considering supporting another, and we have asked the Deans' Council for three more.

Our intent in choosing them so far in advance of the fall semester was that we would be able to train them in preparation of fall duties. We set up an organizational scheme whereby an Executive Committee consisting of the director of the Noel Studio (Rusty) and the co-directors of the Teaching and Learning Center (Hal and Charlie) served as facilitators of a professional learning community (see our previous posts). The Committee created all the original documents that explained the Faculty Innovator to our overseers, the Deans' Council—the overview of the Faculty Innovators Program, the job description of a Faculty Innovator, an even the Faculty Innovator Coordinator (one FI is chosen each year to serve as a liaison between the Executive Committee and the Innovators, and to be in charge of such things as setting up meetings). During the summer and at the beginning of the fall semester, the Executive Committee facilitated bi-weekly meetings of the PLC, a job we then turned over to the FI Coordinator.

What Do the Faculty Innovators Do?

In our job description of Faculty Innovators, we suggested some minimal requirements and tasks that all should be able to perform:
- Attend regular meetings and professional development sessions.
- Provide one presentation/year as part of our Teaching & Learning Initiative.
- Facilitate one PLC (i.e., PLC, Breakfast & a Book, Creative Community/year, including keeping records of such things as attendance, who presents what).
- Work at our August orientations (i.e., full-time faculty, part-time faculty, first-year course instructors, and teaching assistants), including introducing oneself and the FI program at the initial College meeting of the year.
- Provide individual class observations.
- Offer specialized workshops for colleges, departments, and programs.
- Maintain a record of all activities.
- Help with each end-of-the-semester assessment.
- Help train the incoming class of FIs.
- Work in the new Faculty Innovator Training Studio.

Sound interesting? Next time we'll continue with the Faculty Innovator Program, detailing the specifics of budget, how FIs are selected, maneuvering in the political climate, and some tips on success.

Tips for Implementation

A. Select faculty from across campus to represent their colleges or departments.

B. Open up a nominating process to gather input from all faculty at your institution.

C. Recruit colleagues with different strengths and experience levels, including peer observation, technology, information literacy and research, pedagogy, and other areas focused on aspects of teaching and learning.

D. Seek faculty members with a diverse range of personalities and interests, including those in different ranks from first-year tenure-track Assistant Professors to senior-level Professors.

Discussion Questions

A. What opportunities do faculty have at your institution to propose and discuss innovative approaches to teaching and learning?

B. How might you discuss the potential benefits of a cross-campus team of faculty focused on teaching and learning with a colleague or senior administrator?

Activities

A. Assemble a chart that includes in the first column a list of colleges or departments at your institution. In the second column, list teaching backgrounds, experiences, and expertises that you would value in your ideal program. Next, identify at least one faculty member from each department to fit those roles.

B. Map the colleges or departments at your institution in a quick sketch. What would each offer to support the exchange of innovative ideas to enhance teaching and learning?

2. Behind the Scenes with Wizards Behind the Faculty Innovators

(Posted 13 January 2016)

http://newforums.com/the-wizards-behind-the-faculty-innovators/

Just as Oz couldn't function without the wizard behind the scenes, so our Faculty Innovators Program—discussed in the previous post—could not operate without the guidance of an **Executive Committee** (EC). As mentioned before, we have a three-person EC, consisting of the director of the Noel Studio and the two co-directors of the Teaching & Learning Center.

The key to the EC is contained in another previous post called "Tuesday Morning" (where interestingly we refer to how "we had to prepare a final draft for a program we call Faculty Innovators"); here, we detailed how for the past four years the three of us have set up a regular meeting. To recapitulate, we hold a weekly meeting (Tuesdays) at the same time (now 8:00-9:30 as we have to adjust for semester schedules) with an agenda that each of us has constructed during the week (Charlie, for instance, keeps a note pad on his desk where he jots down ideas during the week that need a group discussion, while Rusty prefers to record his items on his Mac). While not all of our conversation revolves around the Faculty Innovators program, we have noticed that in this the first semester of its actuality, 25% of our Tuesday meetings is devoted to operating this program. What do we discuss?

Vision. The entire Faculty Innovators Program was born of a brainstorming session, so it is quite appropriate that we continue elaborating on that vision. Right now, for instance, Tuesday's EC meetings have focused on what documents we need both for the perpetuation of the FI program and for administrators such as deans and our provost to be able to obtain. A few weeks ago we created job descriptions for the Faculty Innovators and the FI Coordinator, placing both on our FI website (the subject of an upcoming post). Why, you ask, didn't we start the entire program with such descriptions? We did, but since so much of this program is a "learn by going where you have to go" process, we have constantly updated our descriptions from last spring with new details as the actualities of the job unfold.

Assessment. As the semester nears its end, we need evidence of our program's effect upon the faculty. Along the way, we have collected necessities such as attendance records and actual consultations performed as well as inventing certificates to hand out to faculty for their professional development records. A while ago we developed an assessment form that is sent to each PLC participants. All this data tell us we need to continue to design and implement faculty development—programming representative of the teaching and learning on campus and where we would like to go in the future with pedagogy, collaboration, and technology, for example.

Retreat. In early January before the spring semester begins, we need everyone to come together. Our main job will be to analyze the data so as to send a report to our superiors. Having all the FIs present ensures their data are available, and we have many points of view to brainstorm our conclusions. Specifically, as with every FI meeting, we will use Google documents to write and record our conversation. We also have to train the group periodically. This January, for instance, we will be starting classroom observation strategies.

Teaching & Learning Innovations Series. Every semester we post on multiple sites our schedule of workshops and other events. Some of these events are generated in our bi-weekly FI meetings that we plan with the FI Coordinator, but the bulk of them come from the three of us. We present them at the next FI meeting and allow for elaboration, the choosing of a date for the workshop, a blurb about it, and the choice of a facilitator. We also try to align these workshops with our so-called milestone events (discussed in a previous post)—New Faculty Orientation, the Provost's Speaker Series, Scholarship Week, and Pedagogicon 2016.

Delivery Platform. At the moment, because of our "learn by going where we have to go" process, we do not have a single platform to serve as a repository of everything we do. The FIs do have a website, but right now it's mostly for internal use of the FIs, not the faculty. We have a You Tube channel with at the moment only three videos. We also have a proprietary website on BlackBoard called MENTOR that allows us to deliver our modular training (all new and part-time faculty, for instance, are given access to our one-hour module on College Teaching, which they must complete before the end of the fall semester—something else that becomes part of our assessment. What we need, however, is one, simplified platform for all faculty. For that, the provost has convened a cross-campus committee to investigate what can and should be done. Rusty convenes that committee, so whatever we discuss on Tuesdays, we know is brought to the committee.

Writing. The entire Faculty Innovator experience is the subject of a book we're writing. Guess who the editors and chief writers are?

Day-to-Day Matters. Somebody has to go to each PLC facilitator to find out what resources are needed—books, food, research. Somebody has to oversee whether the PLCs and workshops actually meet and whether records of these events are turned in. Somebody has to preview these books as to cost and appropriateness. Somebody has to keep track of the budget and how we are progressing with allotted funds throughout the year. We also facilitate a Creative Community (CC)—which meets bi-weekly through the fall, winter, spring and summer terms—has evolved into fiction writers actually writing and publishing books. Somebody has to figure out how to evaluate the CC; in all cases that "somebody" is the Executive Committee.

Tips tor Implementation

A. Even though your program might not have adequate funding for multiple personnel, identify several individuals across campus (beyond your advisory board) whose opinion you value, and call on them for insights into various issues that arise.

B. Be constantly searching for possible collaborations with other units across campus that might aid you in decision-making for implementing your initiatives.

Discussion Questions

A. How "hands on" do you want to be relative to your program's initiatives?

B. Do you have enough campus cred and strong relationships to partner with other units?

Activities

A. Invite several key colleagues from across campus for coffee and brainstorming sessions about possible directions in faculty development.

B. Set up regular meetings with your staff to get their insights on your program, and solicit possible initiatives from them.

3. How to Select Faculty Innovators

(Posted 20 January 2016)

http://newforums.com/how-to-select-faculty-innovators/

For the past few posts, we've been discussing **Faculty Innovators**, those selected faculty members who bring development to the campus. An interesting question involves how they are selected. After all, they don't fall out of trees.

Actually, they sort of do. Remember the 1989 movie *Field of Dreams* where Kevin Costner hears the whispering, "If you build it, he will come"? Centers of Teaching & Learning (CTLs) have enjoyed a similar phenomenon. If you build a CTL, faculty will show—but too few of them. However, those few who show up for every event and try to enroll in every Professional Learning Community (PLC) will be dedicated, and it's from this cream you can find a few good people.

In short, in the beginning, choosing Faculty Innovators is almost a self-selecting process. A CTL wants to recruit faculty who are passionate about pedagogy, and what better litmus test than participation in CTL events?

Our selection process has two stages. For the first two years of our Faculty Innovators program, stage one, we wanted the absolute best, most interested faculty—that is, we wanted to select those who have been selecting us. We have been building this program on the fly, and we didn't want to stop to create a selection rubric, nor did we want to have to spend the time in the beginning dealing with faculty who had not shown a previous interest in development.

One way we recruited was to look back through our events for recurring participants. Of course, some faces stood out because we had worked closely with them and had gotten to know them well. Years ago, for instance, we ran a Learning Environment for Academia's Future (LEAF) program, wherein we brought faculty in during the summer to an experimental classroom and trained them in its technology as well as best pedagogical practices. The next semester we had these LEAF fellows teach a class in this classroom, we observed them several times, and we conferenced with them afterwards. We also met with them at various times during the year as part of a PLC. One of our first choices was a graduate of this program who had actually published an article about LEAF.

Another choice had come to us with an idea for a PLC on cultural competency. With our help he had even developed a book proposal on this subject that was eventually picked up by New Forums. A third selection had not only run PLCs for us on metacognition and deep learning, but was his department's pedagogical coordinator. Still another ran the Women and Gender Studies program and, since she once had had an office next to us, we had mentored. Another choice had offered to run a PLC for us, while another had not only attended many sessions and facilitated a PLC, but dwelt in a college on the other side of the campus. Years ago another colleague had worked with us on the Quality Enhancement Program as a coach. As she was retiring at the end of this year, she said she would meet with the Innovators and consult with her dean on her replacement, who then joined us this year.

Our plan, then, is not to use a formal selection process for this year and the next. After all, we are still ironing out the creases. In the meantime, the Executive Committee with input from the current FIs is developing a selection rubric for stage two that we ought to be implementing about this time next year. When done, the process will call for interested applicants to apply online, have their applications read by the current FIs, and be chosen by April. Each year during Scholarship Week (held the second week in April), we present the upcoming FIs to the University at large.

So far our embryonic rubric has produced a few standards:

- At least one FI must be from each of the five colleges. Because it is the largest on campus, the College of Arts and Sciences needs two Faculty Innovators.
- Applicants who have volunteered to facilitate PLCs or present workshops and have demonstrated excellence will be given preference.
- Preference will be accorded those with pedagogical experience—e.g., teaching such a course, serving as departmental pedagogy coordinator, or attending/presenting at pedagogical conferences like the Lilly or our own Pedagogicon.
- Preference will be given to applicants who have won departmental, college, university, or even state/national awards for teaching.

In short, we're looking for leaders, alphas, people with initiative.

If you're interested in our public website on the Faculty Innovator Program, check out http://studio.eku.edu/facultyinnovators.

Tips for Implementation

A. Be aware of those faculty members who regularly participate in faculty development events. They not only form your "choir," but are potential presenters, facilitators, and even Faculty Innovators.

B. Monitor campus news to identify faculty members who are actively publishing and presenting at conferences.

C. Keep a list of those faculty members who have won awards or have been recognized for achievement. Consider sending them congratulatory texts/emails.

Discussion Questions

A. Do you have a working relationship with a majority of programs across campus? When new people assume leadership roles in these organizations, do you contact them?

B. Have you thought about a comprehensive program of development that could include a group such as the Faculty innovators? What training would be needed?

Activities

A. Create a rubric for Faculty Innovator qualifications.
B. Investigate possible incentives for the program.

4. An Inside Look at a Faculty Innovator Progress, Part I

Posted 3 February 2016

http://newforums.com/inside-look-at-a-faculty-innovator-progress-part-1/

Traditionally, when groups go to a non-work area for a day of training, the event is called a retreat. Since the word retreat carries negative connotations—especially as a military term meaning to fall back—we always describe our one-day workshops as progresses, a noun that always suggests a movement forward, a journey to a goal.

One goal of the Faculty Innovator (FI) Executive Committee (three unit directors plus the FI Coordinator) is to establish professional development sessions. After all, in all the official documents on our website, FIs are referred to as "trained." The main problem in training our cadre revolves around a suitable time all are free. During the fall semester, we held bi-weekly, one-hour meetings, but these sixty-minute sessions usually concentrated on distributing key information and putting out the fire of the moment rather than actually learning how to accomplish something like a peer observation.

A comprehensive examination of free six-hour blocks for FIs during the semester obviously concluded such periods did not exist. What we learned is that really only two good training times for such blocks exist: sometime during the summer and in the two-week period after the holiday break and before the start of the spring semester. Unfortunately, we used last summer's window mostly for an organizational meeting, so our only training came in early January.

Our Executive Committee met twice in early January to set the agenda. The topics were easy to discover; the hard part consisted of creating the proper environment. In a recent episode of the TV show *Limitless*, the hero, Brian, puts on a training session for his FBI handlers in a way he considers interesting by using a makeshift storyboard with a mobile (as over a baby's crib). Unimpressed, the female head of the FBI smugly reminds him, "We do have PowerPoint." The point is that so many training sessions we have attended in the past five years have depended heavily on PowerPoint, and as great believers in "PowerPoint promotes passivity," we wanted to avoid that technology and give our FIs a fun event that demanded active learning. Not only did a six-hour session demand engagement to keep them there the entire time, but we wanted to reinforce non-passive learning paradigms.

As a result, we came up with the following agenda:

8:45-9:00	Meet, Greet, and Eat (we provided a healthy breakfast)
9:00-9:05	Welcome/Preview of Goals
9:05-10:05	Envisioning the Role of the FI
10:05-10:15	Break
10:15-11:15	15-Minutes to Innovation (short modules for web PD)
11:15-12:00	Lunch and Video Interviews

By Charlie Sweet, Hal Blythe & Russell Carpenter

12:00-1:00	Best Practices for Faculty Consultation
1:00-2:00	Best Practices for Peer Observation of Teaching
2:00-2:10	Break
2:10-2:35	Faculty Development in the College and Department
2:35-3:00	Debrief

But, as we noted earlier, the key wasn't what we did, but how we did it. We started with the FI Coordinator facilitating a group discussion wherein all ten participants brainstormed the characteristics of the ideal FI. As the group called out roles, one of the Executive Committee served as scribe, listing the roles on a flip chart. We then repeated the process with the question: what accomplishments define a good FI candidate? The ten FIs were then grouped into five pairs, who were asked to determine the top three roles of FIs. As in speed-dating, they were re-paired to consider the top three items the campus needs from FIs. Eventually everyone reported out, with the items on the flip charts receiving each pair's votes. The result was a refinement of FI duties.

The most popular exercise came after the break. Each person was given a packet of Post-Its, asked to list the five most critical pedagogical strategies (one/Post-It), and encouraged to place the Post-Its on a white board. The Post-Its were then regrouped in columns so that the FIs could tell instantly which Post-Its proved the most popular. The FIs were re-paired and given twenty minutes to create the outline of a video module on the subject and, using materials given them in the middle of the room, were asked to create a low-res prototype that embodied the essence of their module. Each team then, using their prototype, pitched its module. The winner got to write a script for their video that we will actually create this semester and place on our professional development on demand channel, the Faculty Innovator Network.

Next time we'll go into what else happened to make our progress such a resounding success.

5. An Inside Look at a Faculty Innovator Progress, Part II

(Posted 11 February 2016)

http://newforums.com/inside-look-at-faculty-innovator-progress-part-ii/

Last time we discussed what made the morning of our January progress such a success. After an excellent lunch, we moved onto a two-hour afternoon session. Our lunch served a double-duty purpose. First, we had it catered from the local Panera with plenty of options in sandwiches, salads, and drinks (a full FI is a productive FI). Second, while most participants were eating, we sent out one FI at a time for a five-minute filmed interview with our Media Producer. Each FI's answers to such questions as "Why did you want to be an FI?" to "What has been your most rewarding moment as an FI?" were captured by camera to be inserted on the Faculty Innovator website so as to personalize each participant.

Our first afternoon session dealt with their most common role, being a faculty consultant. First, we brainstormed what we considered best practices in offering faculty consultations. That list was reduced to what the group considered the five best practices. With those practices as background guidelines, we moved on to four scenarios. The re-paired teams were given a slip of paper with a scenario in which a faculty member came with a problem, and they had to supply their best response. Each team presented how they would handle the problem; afterwards, the other FIs provided some alternate ways of dealing with the situation.

For instance, one team was handed a scenario (written by the Executive Committee) in which an Associate Professor, concerned about class participation, confessed that he called on the most willing to talk, but never had 100% participation. Was 100% a good goal? How do you keep alpha students involved, yet provide an opportunity for others to talk? How do you draw out the painfully shy? How do you handle the unprepared? Should one allow the law school "I pass"? The team's response, as well as the comments by the other FIs, was checked against our list of best practices. As a result, some best practices were modified by the experience, while other best practices had to be added. What stood out for us was the camaraderie and the compassion displayed.

The second hour focused on the best practices for peer observation of teaching. Recently, we have seen an increase in the number of faculty requesting a classroom observation, a three-part process that includes a pre-conference to determine the goals of the observation (e.g., Do I build rapport? Am I organized? Do I overdo the technology), the actual observation, and the follow-up conference. Traditionally, the Teaching & Learning Center (TLC) has handled these observations because the co-directors have been trained and are very experienced, but lately more and more faculty have been in need (the Blythe-Sweet Law of Classroom Observation says that observations arise in direct proportion to promotion and tenure demands), and the TLC has needed help.

To prepare for the session, the FIs were previously provided with a notebook containing (among other things) the observation rubric we use and were asked to read an article placed in the FI Dropbox (a future post will cover how the FIs use technology). Once again, we reviewed/brainstormed the best practices for the process, and we even created a list of taboos. At that point the group was presented some scenarios and asked to come up with possible solutions. This time members worked alone, then presented their ideas to the group. A subsequent discussion refined and increased our best practices. This subject is so important for the campus that we are running a professional learning community on peer observation this spring.

Each section was designed to be facilitated by a different member of the four-person Executive Committee to offer a variety of styles. In practice what happened was that no matter who led, the other three jumped right in.

In the final section we covered successes and failures in disseminating innovation to the deans, colleges, and departments. FIs fessed up to things they could have done better and proudly proclaimed their successes. At the end we were able to synthesize our procedures into things we should do and things we should not do. We also rearranged our spring meetings to be every three weeks (vs. two in the fall) and set up a Doodl poll for best times.

Ultimately, two major things contributed to the success of the progress. First, we had selected excellent FIs, who were not only very good at what they do, but were also superb communicators as well as creative and critical thinkers. Second, we had spent sufficient time in preparation so that we had a three-page, single-space outline that listed even the smallest of details (e.g., how much coffee to order, materials needed, and a who-will-do-what list).

Tips for Implementation (Parts I & II)

A. Carefully plan a progress well in advance in order to have time for checks and double checks of the agenda.

B. Plan for an active learning session rather than a static PowerPoint presentation.

C. Make the sessions two-way, encouraging Faculty Innovators to contribute their unique ideas and visions.

D. Carve out time for the Innovators to interact informally so that the event is enjoyable as well as informative.

Discussion Questions

A. What is it you hope to achieve by bringing the Innovators together?

B. How open are you to new ideas and directions that might result from the event?

C. Have you considered effective assessment of the event and effective follow-up (i.e., who will do what when)?

Activities

A. Survey the Innovators for ideas on activities for the event and value their input.

B. Administer an effective assessment tool to capture the Innovators' evaluations of the event.

6. Using Technology to Build the Faculty Innovation Network

(Posted 17 February 2016)

http://newforums.com/using-technology-build-the-faculty-innovator-network/

In explaining the creation of the Faculty Innovators, that group of faculty trained in consultations and workshops who are sent to various colleges and departments around campus, we emphasized our primary motivation in their *raison d'etre* was that since faculty would not come to us for professional development, we would go to them. Remember, at our traditional workshops, presentations, and communities (professional learning, creative, and Breakfast and a Book), over a ten-year period, each year we were attracting only 10% of the faculty.

But, we realized, the establishment of the Faculty Innovators was by itself an insufficient solution to the lack of participation problem. Technology offered us another way to bring the development to our faculty. After all, even the busiest of faculty will spend ten minutes watching videos of dogs tobogganing down a ski slope or binge-watching *Homeland*. In fact, our local cable company with its "on-demand" capability helped provide a model for what we called "PD On Demand."

Our foray into using technological programming actually began quite differently. For years the administration has been looking for a cost-effective way of training faculty pedagogically. After all, our university's theme is "Excellence in Teaching Is Job 1." Every year at New Faculty Orientation, we spent an entire day presenting a workshop on the best practices in teaching for our newbies. Unfortunately, we had groups slipping through the cracks who remained untrained in pedagogy—mid-season hires and part-time faculty. How could we catch those groups?

Several years ago for our Ed.D. program in Educational Leadership, we had helped the College of Education develop a course, EDL 830 College Teaching, which covered the best practices. One solution, then, for those falling through the pedagogical cracks was to enroll them in that course. Unfortunately, the College of Education did not have the personnel to teach that many sections, nor did the University want to defray the tuition cost of enrolling so many people.

Our next solution was **MENTOR**, the Modular Educational Network for Training with Online Resources. Essentially, we reduced the 16-week, three-hour course to a one-hour interactive module that we placed on our university's course-management system, Blackboard, and we enrolled all new full-time and part-time instructors at the University. Functioning similarly to those training videos on Title IX that the University requires of everyone, MENTOR even provided a test for the users to complete. Anyone scoring 80% received a downloadable certificate and became part of our permanent record of MENTOR graduates.

MENTOR was just the beginning because it painted pedagogy in broad strokes only. We needed to be able to fill in the gaps. Our unit received permission to hire a Media Producer, and we began to develop videos for what we called the Faculty Innovator Network (FIN). Before even scripting started, we developed some guidelines for effective instructional videos:

1. **Brevity**: having read John Medina's *Brain Rules* (Seattle: Pear Press, 2008), we were very conscious that short attention spans are found in professors as well as students. Therefore, we decided to keep all our videos short and as far under the fifteen-minute attention span as we could. This brevity was also shaped by professor's schedules; even the busiest instructor can find ten minutes to view something beyond cute, cuddly kittens.

2. **Sharp Focus**: over the past year, having reviewed conference proposals, submissions for two books in our "It Works for Me" series, and proposals for the *Journal of Faculty Development*, we have discovered how difficult it is for scholars to focus on their thesis. Our videos would simplify and synthesize the material and center on what Gerry Nosich in *Learning to Think Things Through* (Upper Saddle River, NJ: Pearson, 2009) calls "fundamental and powerful concepts."
3. **Strong Visuals**: in *Brain Rules* Medina also emphasizes that vision trumps the other senses: "If information is presented orally, people remember about ten percent, tested 72 hours after exposure. That figure goes up to 65% if you add a picture" (234). Therefore, we wanted authentic images that would core their way into instructors' brains.
4. **Interest**: anything we shot, we wanted to connect to major professorial interests.

Our first product for the Faculty Innovator Network looked like an MTV video. It ran less than four minutes, focused on the demographics of the typical EKU student, contained actual students, administrators, and alums during homecoming holding up signs during a parade, at a football game, and sitting in our ravine that emphasized such things as "50% of students work part-time." Underlying the visuals was a catchy tune. Interestingly, we found faculty and students sometimes watched the video just to see who was in it. As former English instructors, we used to constantly talk about the importance of knowing your audience (something Communication also stresses), so we also used the video at New Faculty Orientation both to help our newbies get a sense of our student body and to introduce them to a new pedagogical tool, the Faculty Innovator Network.

Next time we'll discuss some problems we have had, other videos shot and in progress, and where we hope to go with the FIN.

Tips for Implementation

1. Do your best to find a media consultant or an instructional designer. Otherwise, you are severely limited by what you don't know.

2. Once again, networking around campus can find you the help you need.

Discussion Questions

1. Some people believe that technology is a mere fad. Do you think videos have real value in teaching and learning beyond the simple appeal to the tech generation?

2. In a recent article in the *Wall Street Journal* (11 July 2016), a law professor admitted that once he started observing colleagues' classes from the rear with a full view of distracted future LLBs watching videos and playing games on their laptops, he subsequently banned them from his classroom. If you make a video, are you willing to watch your students watch it? In short, should any video be assessed not only by its users but by its makers?

Activities

1. Make any video. Keep it short and simple. Think of it as a beta version. Remember that no risk, no reward. Shoot it on your iPhone if you must.

2. Take the video to a professional, tell him/her what was your intent with it, and ask for help.

7. Funding the Faculty Innovator Program

(Posted 3 August 2016)

http://newforums.com/funding-the-faculty-innovators-program/

Background

Dee Fink of *Creating Significant Learning Experiences* (2003) fame has championed Centers for Teaching and Learning (CTLs) in his books, articles, and appearances at national conventions and campuses across the country. One of his key ideas is that CTLs should be funded at the rate of 1-1.5% of the total salaries of that university's faculty, and if the CTL is charged with developing teaching assistants, part-time faculty, and other groups (e.g., first-year course instructors), their salaries should be included in the calculation. We can hear the laughter in response to Dee's dictum from here, and we echo your scoffing.

CTLs are traditionally one of the most under-funded units on any campus. If our budget were one-tenth of Dee's suggestion, our implementation could fulfill our imagination. The hard, cold reality is that CTLs must do more with less, for despite the pressure on colleges and universities from their accrediting agencies to demonstrate true faculty development, most of us inside the CTLs spend our lives eking out a meager existence, begging deans and provosts for money, and having to perform all the jobs we can't pay someone else to do.

So when we began the **Faculty Innovators** (FIs) program, our big worry wasn't that we were starting before we had the whole thing figured out, but rather that while we believed we had a brilliant concept for reaching those 90% of the faculty who would not come by our CTL (but nevertheless need faculty development), we were still missing one thing—funding. How much money did we figure a program consisting of people—Faculty Innovators—and programming—the Faculty Innovation Network—would cost?

Costs–Personnel

We began with the obvious. While we were going to have to do a lot of additional work administering the program, we were not going to see one more penny in our bi-weekly paycheck, but we were going to have to hire additional personnel. Our figures were based on our working for a 16,000-student regional comprehensive with three doctoral programs and five colleges. In terms of personnel, here's what we projected:
- Media Specialist

- Instructional Designer
- Faculty Innovator Coordinator (i.e., one release per year)
- (9) Faculty Innovators (i.e., one release/year/person).

We have deliberately left out the actual costs as the amounts will vary a great deal depending upon the size of the school, the location, and union contracts. At our institution, we would figure that the cost of paying someone else to teach a three-hour course at approximately $2600, so all ten would cost the University $26,000. In our case we hired a full-time media specialist (to produce videos for our PD On Demand system), but we settled this first year for one-quarter of an instructional designer's time for one semester. Moreover, other personnel costs aren't figured in as we use a graduate assistant and two administrative assistants (AA) for a small portion of time both for our primary and our FI workload. Just this morning, for instance, we had an AA place a notice on the campus email system about a PLC to be held next semester. A guesstimate of our total personnel expenses would be around $70,000.

Costs—Non-Personnel

So much of what we use for the Faculty Innovators is part of the campus environment. For instance, the group met this morning in the Faculty Lounge, which is free. We utilized our unit's projector that threw a Google Docs document upon the TLC's white screen. We didn't have to pay for heat or electricity, and the three of us supplied two pots of free coffee.

We have yet to subscribe to a journal, but even there we have an in. Rusty is the incoming editor of the *Journal of Faculty Development*. While we have a digital repository for key FI documents and the Faculty Innovator Network, occasionally we make copies of reprinted articles or someone's workshop to distribute to the FI notebooks (which we got free because they were left over from New Faculty Orientation).

Our big non-human expense has been for books for our Professional Learning Communities (PLCs). We run three PLCs/semester, and we encourage each PLC facilitator to choose at least one book. Last semester, for example, our How learning Works facilitator chose two, costing over $30 per paperback X 2 X n15 PLC members. Right there we spent around $3000. And occasionally we serve food as in our each-semester retreats. Sometimes we pay for travel to local, regional, or national conferences.

As you can see, the annual cost for the program might be $100,000. On the other hand, a program that reaches every faculty member . . . priceless.

Tips for Implementation

A. Consult with your supervisor to determine if a Faculty Innovators program is feasible in terms of funding. Be sure to have some cost estimates in hand.

B. Investigate the possibility of financial support from other sources such as deans or even outside grants.

C. Check with your counterparts at other institutions to gain their insights into possible funding sources.

Discussion Questions

A. Is a program such as the Faculty Innovators worth the cost at your institution?

B. Are you willing to sacrifice other programs if necessary to fund the Faculty Innovators?

Activities

A. Do a preliminary cost analysis of a Faculty Innovators program on your campus?

B. Gauge the willingness of funding sources to support a Faculty Innovators program in a suitable fashion.

C. Start small. Our first Innovator we called a Faculty Fellow, and he performed classroom observations around campus for us.

B. Determining Services for Individuals

1. Faculty Development: Consultation and Classroom Observation

(Posted 4 November 2015)

http://newforums.com/faculty-development-consultation-and-classroom-observation/

Years ago before our university even had a CTL, it ran a faculty consultation process. One faculty member directed a cadre of consultants, and each of six consultants worked with two faculty members over sixteen weeks to improve the quality of one's instruction. Unfortunately, the funding dried up, and faculty became disenchanted with devoting an entire semester to intense observing, consulting, formal assessments, and even videotaping, so the program ended.

Most lists of current services offered by CTLs billboard consultation and classroom observation. While the service is valuable, administrators, especially chairs, occasionally view it like hospital triage—please fix my "broken" faculty member. Sometimes these services are performed for entire departments, but most often a trained CTL specialist talks with an individual about pedagogical matters, serving as a coach.

Mini-Consultations

Now we provide what we call mini-consultations. Most faculty don't want to spend a lot of time working on their teaching no matter how much they have been encouraged by chairs, promotion and tenure committees, and even deans. They are willing, however, to devote a small amount of time out of personal interest or academic survival. Most often faculty needing help have identified a specific problem they wish to work on. They start with an email or by simply dropping in. Some faculty hang around after a workshop to ask for specific advice about one aspect of their teaching. Occasionally, we will be visited by a chair who has a faculty member whose assessment scores (we use the IDEA form) are not up to par.

While consultation and observation are most often connected, they are not always so. Recently, we had a faculty member drop in to chat about the whole idea of deep learning. We offered a general explanation and even gave her a book explaining some step that help students learn deeply. When another faculty member asked about the same problem, we saw the writing on the wall. The next semester we provided a professional learning community on the topic.

Classroom Observations

Classroom observations are more complex as they usually demand three steps:
1. Initial Meeting
2. Actual Observation
3. Follow-up Conversation.

In the **initial meeting** the CTL specialist talks with the faculty member to determine what the instructor wants. Some faculty are very specific. One of our earliest such experiences was visiting the class of a professor who specialized in question & answer active learning but had little wait time after his questions. We actually timed the responses and found them less than seven seconds. The initial meeting also establishes any secondary concerns and sets up a specific class time to visit.

For the **actual observation** we have evolved a rubric that we provide to the instructor beforehand. We developed our rubric by starting with Chism's *Peer Review of Teaching* (1999), moving to an experimental classroom, developing a rubric through a professional learning community, and finally synthesizing all our research into *Achieving Excellence in Teaching* (2014). In fact, that book became a self-help guide because we built in an assessment structure we call R.A.T.E.—a Rubric for Achieving Teaching Excellence. At the end of the book we even provide an appendix with rubrics available for selves, colleagues, and students, evaluating everything from an instructor's disposition to his/her ability to teach creatively.

One tip we should suggest for evaluators is be the first to arrive at the observed class and the last to leave. Strike up conversations with students. One of the biggest problems with classroom observations is they tend to provide snapshots of the instructor, and as an observer you want to know how regular are the practices and techniques you are watching. Gaining the trust of the students allows you to ask about the typicality of what you just observed and make better judgments about their typicality.

Even the best trained observers need to be reminded of other potential flaws in the system beyond their own bias (e.g., prejudice against any form of lecture). The Hawthorne Effect recognizes that those being knowingly observed will modify their behavior toward what is perceived as what the observer wants. Of course, if that new pedagogy is positive, then the teacher's behavior is being modified effectively. Sometimes called the Heisenberg Effect, the principle states that the very act of being observed changes the normal dynamics. Our feeling is that if both the observer and observed are aware of these problems, something positive can still be gained.

In the **follow-up conversation** the observer details what has been learned about why the observer was there—e.g., are my classroom presentations organized? Almost always more is learned than what one was looking for. In fact, after thirty years of classroom observations we have learned several things:

- In an active learning era too many faculty rely on class-long lectures.
- Almost no faculty member is truly organized (see our article on keeping it C.R.I.S.P.).
- No faculty member is such an effective teacher that s/he cannot learn something from being observed.
- More than half of those observed don't really like another authoritative presence in their classroom (Ego? Academic freedom? Inability to collaborate?).
- After only five minutes in a classroom, a trained observer can make a fairly accurate judgment on the overall effectiveness of the observed faculty member.

In short, we have found that much can be accomplished in a minimum of contact with faculty if consultation and observation are well designed and executed.

Tips for Implementation

A. Publicize that your program of consultation and classroom observation is both voluntary and confidential in order to combat with the perception that your program operates as a pedagogical hospital designed to "fix" bad teachers.

B. Provide generous windows for scheduling both consultations and observations.

C. Provide a comfortable atmosphere for the initial consultation, and do more listening than talking.

D. Concentrate on a couple of pedagogical areas rather than trying to cover the entire spectrum of concerns.

Discussions Questions

A. Have you developed enough credibility and trust to encourage faculty members to participate in a consultation-observation process?

B. Do you feel confident to work one-on-one with individuals and give them honest criticism?

C. Are you current on the best practices in classroom teaching?

D. Do you have the knowledge, skills, and willingness to work with online teachers?

Activities

A. After researching the field, develop an initial, workable rubric for classroom observation.

B. Open channels for publicizing this aspect of your overall faculty development program.

C. Consider forming a Professional Learning Community to develop a best practices in classroom observation rubric.

2. The Heisenberg Effect: A Flaw in Classroom Observation

(Posted 21 July 2015)

http://newforums.com/flaw-classroom-observation/

As any self-respecting Trekkie or casual follower of the Star Trek TV-movie enterprise knows, the Prime Directive forbids interference in developing civilizations (e.g, don't lose your phaser among stone-age savages on Planet X). As faculty developers who have evaluated over 1000 classes, we've always tried to uphold the prime directive for classroom observation as much as possible. Yet, the longer we observe, the more we've come to believe we interfere.

Usually when we observe, we have already met with the professor and determined some key pedagogical issues the professor desires us to treat. Traditionally we arrive early and slink to the rear of the class, most times without even an acknowledgement of our presence by either the professor or class members. On occasion a professor will introduce us, and some even say why we are there. In any case our role is always determined by the professor's discretion.

Lately we've discovered an interesting phenomenon: the professors we observe seem to be much better teachers than either they or their chairs have led us to believe. They are knowledgeable, interesting, and engaging, and they tend more toward active learning strategies than the usual Sage on the Stage presentations. Why do these teachers appear better than advertised?

We have always had a minimal grasp of the Heisenberg Effect, which states that the mere observation of a thing changes the thing being observed. While faculty development is not the same as particle physics, the principle still speaks to us, informing us that our mere presence alters the behavior of both teacher and student.

In our case, our mere presence seems to ramp up the effort of the teacher as well as the students—they are performing for an audience.

Does the Effect negate the validity of classroom observations? Not necessarily. Anything that bolster's a teacher's performance, if only for a short time, is worthwhile. And certainly making the professor more metacognitive in our reports and our follow-up conferences with the professor is useful.

But is our observation accurate?

We've found one cannot just observe—the whole observation must be placed in a context. Therefore, one of our favorite tactics is to remain in class after the professor has departed--in *Achieving Excellence in Teaching* (2014) we encourage professors wishing to establish rapport to come early and stay late—and engage some of the students in a discussion. If the teacher lingers as we suggest, we simply meet with some students in the hallway. We have one major question: is the class we just observed typical of that professor? This post-class interview provides a check and balance by which we hope to overcome the inherent disadvantage posited by the Heisenberg Effect.

In one memorable post-class interview, students told us that the class we just observed was anything but typical. "Hell," said a student, "it's the only time all semester he's provided us with handouts." Another time a student told us, "He usually stands there in the front and lectures down at us."

Truthfully, we can never overcome the Heisenberg Effect, but we do believe very strongly in expert observation (vs. pure peer observation). Though not perfect, expert observation is necessary to balance an almost crack-like addiction to student evaluations (e.g., IDEA) as the exclusive determiner of professorial competence in the classroom.

By Charlie Sweet, Hal Blythe & Russell Carpenter

Tips For Implementation

A. Even if the instructor has informed the class of your visit, try to be as unobtrusive as possible.

B. Concentrate on one or two aspects of the class.

C. Try to engage a couple of class members before and after the observation to gauge their attitudes about the material and the instructor.

Discussion Questions

A. What is your ultimate goal in observing a class session?

B. Do you believe your presence affects the instructor? The students?

C. Can you think of ways you might turn your presence in the classroom into a positive?

Activities

A. Make a checklist of things to avoid when observing a class.

B. Develop a set of questions you might ask students about the class during an informal chat.

C. Determining Services for Groups: New Faculty, Part-time, First-Year Course Instructors, TAs

By Charlie Sweet, Hal Blythe & Russell Carpenter

1. How to Improve Faculty Attendance at Higher Ed Professional Development Events

(Posted 18 May 2016)

http://newforums.com/how-to-improve-faculty-attendance-at-higher-ed-professional-development-events/

With one week remaining in the semester and one event to go, we are already assured of doubling last year's attendance in our Teaching & Learning Center's professional development program. What did we do to improve campus participation? In truth, it wasn't just one thing, but a combination of them. Of primary importance is the fact that our two-person (we lost an administrative assistant in a reorganization), faculty-facing CTL achieved greater funding and more personnel (a director, a tech, a media producer, and a part-time instructional designer) by merging with another academic unit, the student-facing Noel Studio for Academic Creativity—critical mass.

Of course, increased attendance is not our only goal, but even assessment to evidence value—faculty learning outcomes—can only occur after we've put those faculty bodies in our seats.

Six Super Suggestions

Create a name for your sessions that emphasizes both a continuum of similar events and some aspect of your mission statement. As one of our favorite proverbs states, "The beginning of wisdom is learning to call things by their right names." What had simply been labelled "Roundtables" became the Teaching & Learning Innovation Series (the TLI). "Teaching" and "Learning" obviously reflect our new unit's facing both faculty and students, while "Series" suggests that professional development is more than a potpourri of one-shots, and we appeal to the "Collect the entire set" mentality. Importantly, the new name of the series captures the essence of our unit's mission statement—"Helping Teachers Help Students Learn Deeply"—and allows us to brand or create an identity.

Try to theme your events with something valued by your audience. While the three of us are now primarily administrators, Hal and Charlie began as faculty, while Rusty still is, so we have a good sense of what faculty want as well as need. Since even at a minimum faculty try to stay current with higher education trends, the term "Innovation" implies they are getting things that happened after they left graduate school. In our specific case, the very name of the Noel Studio for Academic Creativity is the basis of innovation. Of course, a theme also unifies professional development.

Establish an electronic registration system. While we never turn away drop-ins, we prefer faculty pre-register for every event. Pre-registration provides a commitment on their part, and a list of participants first gives us an idea of how much material we need for them (e.g., food as well as how many books to order or articles to reprint). Google has made the pre-registration easy, and it provides valuable contact records because we always ask for an email address.

Publicize the events multiple ways. Prepare a base list of events in the semester before the series is held. We always provide physical and virtual copies of the entire schedule during New Faculty Orientation. We advertise the maximum times that our university's daily electronic announcement system allows (in our case, EKU Today). Our pre-registrants receive personal emails about not only an event for which they registered, but every event in the series. Flyers for the next event are handed out to faculty whenever they attend a workshop. At the conclusion of every event, we email our participants a toolkit—a list of resources, exercises, and strategies they can use. Our website lists the events. And Rusty tweets more than the birds flying inside our favorite big box stores, Lowe's and Home Depot.

Utilize a workshop format. If faculty are going to surrender their time, they must feel they are receiving something worthwhile, and they must feel they are taking charge of their learning. Hence, the required active-learning format of workshops satisfies those needs. Most importantly, if we as professional developers are stressing an active-learning, mentor-from-the-middle model of instruction, we had best reinforce that concept at our own workshops. We insist all workshop facilitators employ some activities and interaction. In fact, we have a set of guidelines for facilitators on our website.

Try to use a variety of workshop facilitators. Our first choices are always our Faculty Innovators (about whom we've written much in the past) because they have been selected for their skills and been trained in effective strategies. Our second choice is the three of us, but while we know we can do the job, we'd prefer to solicit others (in fact, the three of us have facilitated our three highest-attended workshops in the TLI Series). For that reason we solicit workshops from faculty and administrators who have contacted us about some pedagogical strategy with which they have had success, and sometimes when the University's every-other-week email comes out with a list of faculty publications and presentations, we solicit those people. Sometimes faculty bring their classes to the Noel Studio for a workshop for their students, get to talking with Rusty about what they are doing, and, voila, a TLI Series event is born.

In short, this year we have focused on reaching more faculty. The TLI Series has done that, but we have found other ways, something we'll discuss in future posts.

Tips for Implementation

A. Whatever the number one subject that faculty want in a professional development event, give it to them.

B. Cull the journals from the *Chronicle of Higher Education* to the *National Teaching & Learning Forum* to discover hot topics. Sometimes faculty aren't aware of what's out there until you help them see it.

Discussion Questions

A. Is the fact that a topic is hot make it right for an event?

B. What is the proper ethic for a faculty developer? What is the middle ground between the "bread and circuses" approach and the very latest neuroscience discovery on teaching and learning?

Activities

A. Try assessing your PD series from two different viewpoints—once by subject and once by presenter. Does anything jump out at you?

B. Consider at least one presentation per semester that's way out there. Sometimes you have to try new things and stretch the minds of your participants.

2. Innovating Faculty Development Lessons from Pedagogy Day

(Posted 13 August 2015)

http://newforums.com/innovating-faculty-development-lessons-from-pedagogy-day/

By far our most important development for faculty development at Eastern Kentucky University (EKU) has been Pedagogy Day. Our last post discussed innovating New Faculty Orientation (NFO) in general, but this post will concentrate on New Faculty Development.

Remember the old Head and Shoulders TV commercial with the tagline "You never get a second chance to make a first impression"? What first impression do you want to make on your new faculty? Perhaps as an R1 institution, you want to stress the importance of scholarship. Our university is an historic teacher's college with a 4-4 teaching load wherein the emphasis has always been on teaching. Therefore, we created a poster for it that reads EXCELLENCE IN TEACHING IS JOB ONE for our website, and appropriately, we labelled it Pedagogy Day.

2 Principles for Innovating the New Faculty Experience: SPACE

We are great believers in Marshall McLuhan's dictum that the medium is the message, so the space in which we hold initial session is as much important as our words. When we first began a decade ago, NFO was held in an ornate lecture hall with the participants lined up in rows and columns; the talking heads stood in from of the room and talked from behind a lectern. What was the overall message if not learning the lecture format? Unfortunately, at the current evolution, active learning had been the dominant pedagogy for 15 years, but the space did not reflect that fact.

The next step was to transition NFO from the ornate lecture space to our Noel Studio for Academic Creativity. The Discovery Classroom consists of a large room with two-floor high ceilings complete with two skylights that admit volumes of sunlight. Instead of rows and columns, the room contains tables on wheels and movable chairs. Interspersed through the room are smartboards, flip charts, computers, and monitors. The wall has been painted bright colors on which hang contemporary art pieces. A spiral staircase that seems a wooden representation of the DNA structure leads to the next floor. As we detail in *Teaching Applied Creative Thinking* (2013) brighter spaces produce deeper thinking students, and brighter spaces are created by four elements:

- Natural light
- Bright colors
- Flexible and comfortable furniture
- Writable spaces (pp. 23-24).

Instructor Placement

If our students—i.e., new professors—have these tools geared toward active learning, where do we place the instructors? Years ago at the Lilly Conference on Teaching & Learning at Miami, we met Erica McWilliam, bought her *The Creative Workforce* (2007), and bought into her theory in effective instructors being meddlers from the middle. In the aforementioned *Teaching Applied Creative Thinking*, we modified her approach to what we call mentor from the middle. As we said there, "The Mentor-from-the-Middle, as a new paradigm for teaching, calls on the instructor to assume several roles: facilitator, coach, artist, critical reflector, model, and scholar" (p. 60).

And do it all from the middle of the room. We also reasoned that if one mentor is good, why not use more, so now on Pedagogy Day the three of us begin in the middle of the Discovery Classroom, and throughout the two-plus hours we circulate throughout the crowd. Not only do we make eye contact, but we constantly touch upon the participant's 18-inch-imaginary cylinder around them. In short, they invaded out physical space, and now we invade their psychological space.

On a theoretical level, having three co-instructors sends a powerful message about **collaboration** (one of our creative thinking strategies) in teaching, something we did for over thirty-five years. On a [practical level, while we have a "script" for Pedagogy Day, so much of what we do is **piggybacking** (another of our creative thinking strategies) off each other's comments as well as those of our newbies. The resulting spontaneity creates a remarkable **flow** (still another of our creative thinking strategies).

Obviously, through our use of space and our instructional methodologt, we are modeling key teaching strateghies. No matter what we say to them, we have found through post-NFO surveys <u>what they most remember is what we do.</u>

3. How to Communicate Best Practices in Higher Ed Pedagogy

(Posted 21 October 2015)

http://newforums.com/how-to-communicate-best-practices-higher-ed-pedagogy/

Last time we explained the importance of space and instructor placement in Pedagogy Day, the opening day of our innovated New Faculty Orientation. But now that we've explained the medium, what is the message? How would you communicate to new faculty the best practices in pedagogy?

Our fundamental and powerful concept here is that it must be modeled, and that is especially true of our mentor from the middle approach. As we say in *Teaching Applied Creative Thinking* (2013), "A body of research has established the efficacy of the mentor as model" (58). Another way of looking at this approach comes from an allied field. As Hal and Charlie point out in their creative writing guidebook, *Options* (2014), showing is a more effective storytelling method than telling, so rather than lecture, we stage a scene.

The three of us begin the workshop in the middle of the room surrounded by tables with eight people sitting at each table. Sitting on a flip chart as the newbies enter the room is a poster bearing the inscription **EXCELLENCE IN TEACHING IS JOB ONE**, which is also at the bottom of every email they have received from us since their hiring. As the mentor from the middle is an active learning approach, we keep lecturing at a minimum (i.e., the mini-lecture) and focus on 1) questions and answers, 2) group work, and 3) reflection.

Questions and Answers

As we start the workshop, here are some of our favorite interactive questions:
1. How many years of experience in college teaching, part-time or full-time, do you have?
2. Have you ever experienced any of the following elements of pedagogical training: supervised training, a graduate course in pedagogy, publication of a SOTL article, or attendance at a pedagogical conference?

A discussion of these questions usually makes the point that few new faculty members have had much professional development.

Next we like another big question: If excellence in teaching is our main job, what's our goal with that teaching? What we aim at through discussion is to get around to the concept of **deep learning**—we want to try to foster learning that endures.

That question is usually followed with another: what can we do as instructors to aid deep learning in our students? The ensuing discussion usually segues into our stressing the importance of the **Four Rs of Deep Learning**:
- **Receive** information

- **R**etrieve Information
- **R**ate information, and
- **R**eflect upon how the new information relates to old knowledge.

Group Work

At this point we get into the meat of our presentation. As research indicates that the most effective learning in group work begins with individual effort, we ask each participant to consider two alliterative questions: what are the top ten attitudes and the top ten strategies for terrific teachers? Each new faculty member must use the paper provided and <u>jot down</u> five answers for each question. Then, we <u>pair & share</u> as everyone must collaborate with one other person at the table to come up with a single top five list for both categories. Finally, the entire table of eight must negotiate with each other and <u>publish</u> their two decided-upon lists on a flip chart we have provided for each table.

Reflection

At this point we have anywhere from five to eight flip charts filled with information. We ask the attendees to take some time to look around at the different lists. Then, using the higher-order Bloom skills of analyzing and evaluating what they see, through frequency or any other research method they deem applicable, create two new top five lists. We then select various members around the room to argue the merits of the traits upon their own new lists. Eventually, we try to build a consensus.

Final Thoughts

Throughout this workshop the three of us constantly circulate around the room, looking in on individuals and groups, making suggestions to help new faculty refine their lists, acting as both advocate and devil's advocate. Sure, we know what the research has shown the top traits to be—we literally wrote not the book, but a book on the subject—but what we are most looking for is engagement, 100% engagement from the group.

Mentoring from the middle, you see, is not just a concept, but an overall methodology that works, and we've found no better way to get this approach across than to model it.

Tips for Implementation (Parts I and II)

A. Determine a venue for New Faculty Orientation that will allow you to model best practices in teaching, including learning environment, instructor placement, and action.

B. Design your presentation with an active learning paradigm, including question and answer, group work, and reflection.

C. Be sure the session calls for New Faculty members to use higher order Bloom skills and that the goal of best practices as deep learning by students is emphasized throughout.

Discussion Questions

A. What are your goals for New Faculty Orientation in terms of pedagogy?

B. How much time should be devoted to treatment of pedagogy during New Faculty Orientation?

C. With what approaches to presentation of pedagogical materials do you feel most comfortable?

Activities

A. Survey available venues on campus to determine which would serve a presentation on pedagogy most effectively.

B. Outline a presentation that will call for both active learning and use of high order Bloom skills by new faculty members.

C. Design your session to provide a take-away for new faculty members that solidifies the presentation's major points.

4. Another Approach to Pedagogy Day

(Posted 11 September 2015)

http://newforums.com/another-approach-to-pedagogy-day/

You might think that with our past two posts being on Pedagogy Day that we had pretty much covered the subject, but innovation has struck again, spurred by necessity. Every year our university expands the population of those needing an introduction to pedagogy, and this year was no exception. In addition to new faculty and new part-time faculty, we were asked to conduct a workshop for instructors of the University's orientation class for undeclared majors and another for graduate students who teach—TAs.

In addition, the more we research pedagogy, the more we realize what a wide field it is. Nine years ago when we taught our first workshop, we focused solely on the top ten strategies for terrific teachers. By 2013 when we were writing our *Achieving Excellence in Teaching: A Self-Help Guide* (2014), we had broadened our pedagogical scope to include not just **Strategies**, but **Dispositions**, a term favored by our co-writer Bill Phillips because of his background in educational research. Recently, in training the instructors of the undeclared majors course, GSD 101, we found ourselves getting into a third category, **Values**, and—again because of research in psychology—even renaming our Dispositions category **Attitudes**.

As we discussed these three categories in a live session last week with new faculty, we found participants questioning how to include all three in a single approach or methodology. Ever innovating, we decided to add a fourth category, **Paradigm**. Moreover, because this week we were facilitating the workshop for TAs, we decided to create a single form that would serve both as a worksheet and their notes. While we could have placed all the needed

information on a single sheet that we just handed them (or crafted a PowerPoint), we knew from research that our best chance for deep learning to occur necessitated several things:
- Participants had to **receive** the information and work on it themselves in trying to understand it (vs. simply being told a la handouts or PowerPoints);
- Participants had to **retrieve** the information as often as possible;
- Participants had to **rate** the new information; and
- Participants had to **reflect** upon the new information.

The Chart

We ended up creating a pedagogical chart that we handed out to the participants at the beginning of the workshop:

EXCELLENT TEACHING

	VALUES	ATTITUDES	STRATEGIES	PARADIGM
1.				
2.				
3.				
4.				
5.				

After bringing up the recent criticism by the Association of American Colleges and Universities (AACU) that graduate schools fail to provide students with pedagogic training, we asked these would-be teachers some research questions of our own:
- How many of you have ever taught before in a supervised program?
- How many of you have attended a pedagogy—not disciplinary—conference?
- How many of you have read a book on pedagogy? Article?
- How many of you have been to a pedagogy event before today?
- How many of you can define pedagogy?

A subsequent discussion on their answers validated the AACU's major point. We then asked each participant to employ **Individual Retrieval** to draw upon his/her positive educational experiences and fill in as many of the fifteen members of the first three columns and five rows as they could. After a few minutes of retrieval, they were asked to **Pair & Share**—i.e., use collaboration with another table member to finish the chart. Finally, we asked each table to select a scribe, discuss the paired charts, and, using an extra EXCELLENT TEACHING form we had provided, come up with a new chart in which the 15 members were ordered as to importance (adding the notion of importance forces the participants not just to list, but to argue for relative worth).

Discussion

Their charts filled, we started by inquiring as to what values were deemed most important; to keep track, we wrote their suggestions on a white board/flip chart. Values such as excellence, honesty, and drive showed up. We repeated the process for attitudes with passion (interesting, enthusiasm), caring, and rapport dominating. The chief strategies followed with organization and setting a high bar receiving the most votes.

As the highest element upon Bloom's revised taxonomy is creating, we next asked them to synthesize the three columns in order to develop a pedagogy. Only a few knew the concept of active learning, but at least the lecture/sage on the stage was not an approach to which they wished to adhere—i.e., they had **rated** the material. We barely had time to introduce the Mentor from the Middle methodology/paradigm before our hour expired.

By that time, however, they had their original EXCELLENT TEACHING form, which they had been revising as we went over the material. In an ideal world we would have had them **reflect** upon what they had learned, but ideal worlds are not created in an hour. However, we do have a survey we can email them that contains some reflective questions.

Tips for Implementation

A. Obviously, we keep tweaking Pedagogy Day. Don't be afraid to make changes, even when you think you are doing your best work. Remember Vince Lombardi's advice that "When you are satisfied, you are through." In other words, keep improving.

B. We made a conscious decision to move from teaching and learning to teaching for deep learning. When in doubt, prefer deep to shallow learning.

Discussion Questions

A. Should all learning be deep? What about for introductory courses in a field? However, when you teach one course for shallow learning and one for deep, how do you think this bifurcation impacts student learning?

B. Do you find rubrics overdone in academia? Necessary?

Activities

A. Do some research on deep learning.
B. Develop one deep learning exercise.

D. Focused Faculty Groups: PLCs, Breakfast & a Books, and Creative Communities

By Charlie Sweet, Hal Blythe & Russell Carpenter

1. Focused Faculty Groups: Breakfast and a Book

(Posted 20 November 2015)

http://newforums.com/focused-faculty-groups-breakfast-and-a-book/

One thing CTLs can do effectively is bring together people from across campus with like interests, especially people who might not otherwise meet. Just as a heart has a diastolic and a systolic purpose, so a good CTL functions as the heart of campus. In our *Introduction to Applied Creative Thinking* (2012), we discuss several advantages of collaboration—participants:

- Increase ideation levels
- Become more sociable
- Generate enthusiasm
- Break down barriers
- Sharpen communication and communication skills, and
- Use others' strengths to compensate for weaknesses (pp. 46-47).

The two collaborations, or focused faculty groups, we have found work the best are the Breakfast and a Book (B&B) and the Professional Learning Community (PLC). We'll discuss the former this time and the latter next time.

Definition

One step above the traditional literary salons, the Breakfast and a Book program is nothing more than a faculty and administrator book discussion group. Obviously any book selected must deal with a significant issue in higher education. After inviting applicants, we usually select 15 from various disciplines as the cross-pollination of reactions from across campus seems important. We choose 15 even though we know an ideal discussion group is smaller because inevitably some folks will drop out. To encourage participation we choose a strong facilitator and book with great appeal. We pay for the books and allow faculty to keep them (as well as the knowledge gained). And because of our faith in a cardinal belief of CTLs—if you feed them, they will come—we supply them with a continental breakfast. B&Bs last a minimum of six weeks, some go on for the entire semester, and some get repeated semester after semester. B&Bs differ from their cousin, Professional Learning Communities, in that no product is demanded. Discussion and reflection are all that is necessary.

When

Years ago we asked the registrar to research the classes at our university in order to discover at what times the faculty are most free—i.e., at what class hour are the fewest classes. The answer came back at the 8:00 and 3:30 class blocks. When we surveyed the faculty, they confirmed the registrar's view and explained that those are the times they are most involved in taking their kids to school and picking them up (our university runs a K-12 laboratory school where buses are not part of the package). We also ran across a study that showed most people experience a significant drop in energy/blood sugar around 3:00 each afternoon. As a result, we figured out the ideal time for a Breakfast and a Book was 8:15, immediately after the kids were dropped at school and the faculty arrived. We've since found that more and more departments are doing away with Friday classes, so the Friday 8:15-9:15 time slot was selected.

Choosing a Book and Facilitator

Every year we put out a call for interested facilitators and books they would like to use. Training a facilitator is easy as we simply lead the first session and let the prospective facilitator learn by watching. Most faculty, especially if they are used to discussion with their classes (vs. pure lecturers), find the facilitator role easy to adapt to. If they have trouble or want help, we'll usually sit in for a longer time. Our office sits off the faculty lounge where B&Bs are held, so we're always around to help.

Recently, for example, the Associate Dean of Graduate Studies became enamored with Sheryl Sandberg's *Lean In* (2013). While the book wasn't based on academia, with its insights on women attaining leadership roles, it certainly was easily applicable to the higher education arena. Another dean, who had become a believer in teaching squares during her prior existence as a faculty member, couldn't find a book on the subject, so she performed some research, then put together a file of significant materials. Fear not, we didn't change the name of the event to Breakfast and Duplicated Copies.

Sometimes we run across an interesting book and ask someone to facilitate a B&B on it. That happened immediately after we read Nicholas Carr's *The Shallows* (2010) about how the Internet has rewired our students' brains and again after the *Chronicle of Higher Education* brought our attention to how little students are learning in Arum & Roksa's *Academically Adrift* (2011). In the future we'd love to run a B&B based on the Heath brothers' *Made To Stick* (2007), which, though centered on politics and advertising, has many applications to postsecondary education.

Why a B&B

A few years ago in one of our B&Bs, the facilitator, who was from loss prevention, and a participant from psychology found through the dialogue that they had some research ideas in common. Since then, we know they have worked on three published collaborations.

In B&Bs everyone learns, and some people learn more and come up with more effective applications of the ideas. And how often do you see faculty and administrators sitting down to talk for an hour?

Tips for Implementation

A. Identify several "hot topics" in culture and academia. These are ideas and concepts faculty and professional staff are reading about individually and discussing with colleagues.

B. Choose or invite colleagues to suggest books that treat some of the topics you have selected.

C. Select a book and advertise the creation of a Breakfast and a Book (B&B) on the topic.

D. Emphasize that the B&B is for discussion and that no product will be expected from the group (as is usually done with a Professional Learning Community).

E. Try for a variety of disciplines when selecting members in order to achieve the broadest perspective and to foster cross-campus collaboration.

F. Emphasize responsibility. If members don't make 2/3s of the B&B's meetings, the book you provided as a gift will be recalled.

Discussion Questions

A. Do you try to keep up with most current trends in academia? Does your CTL subscribe to *The Chronicle of Higher Education* or some similar publication? Do you read the *New York Times* or the *Wall Street Journal* to observe their reporting on higher ed issues?

B. Do you keep an open ear and eye for the latest interests across campus? What are faculty and professional staff discussing? What is on the agenda for your faculty senate? Do you have a liaison with the Deans' Council or Chairs Association?

C. Do you have a library of the latest books and articles on a variety of issues?

D. Do you have a mechanism publicizing upcoming B&Bs, selecting facilitators and members, and even for soliciting suggestions for B&Bs?

E. Does your CTL have adequate funding for books, food, etc.?

Activities

A. Survey faculty and professional staff to identify current issues and interests.

B. Read the most current academic publications to identify the major writers, articles, and books being discussed nationally or internationally? (Hint: check the keynote topics at pedagogical conferences).

C. Check your resources to determine your boundaries in presenting B&Bs in terms of funding, space, time, a compensating facilitators.

2. The Best Center of Teaching and Learning Service for Professional Development

(Posted 4 December 2015)

http://newforums.com/best-center-of-teaching-and-learning-service-professional-development/

A few years ago our state adopted the Common Core Standards and the legislature mandated that all state universities had to align college-level courses to these standards. Our CTL was charged by our university to figure out how to implement Senate Bill 1 on the campus. In short, the problem was: how do we get various groups ranging from math to social sciences to teacher preparation to come together and develop a delivery plan?

Traditional Plcs

Our solution was our go-to process for cross-campus collaboration, the Professional Learning Community. Years ago we attended the Lilly Conference on Teaching and Learning, where we had met Milt Cox (2004), who created the Faculty Learning Community and advocated a few basic principles about his invention:

- Size: 6-15 members
- Frequency: frequent, regular meetings
- Focus: teaching and learning
- Method: active learning principles
- End Product: something tangible to be implemented
- Dissemination: results should be presented to the campus as well as national audience.

Our Brand of PLCs

We always believed that since learning communities can include faculty, administrators, and staff members they should be called Professional Learning Communities. In addition, after a decade of PLC experiences, we've made a few other changes to Cox's principles:

- Size: While 15 members seems high for a successful collaboration (think of brainstorming rules), participants attrit at about a 25% rate, and not everybody shows up for every meeting.
- Frequency: Unless PLCs meet at a two-weeks apart maximum, members will lose interest in even the most compelling subject. Likewise, meeting every week dulls the interest level. Besides, most people are so busy that once every two weeks is about all the time they can give. Two weeks between meetings also gives participants plenty of time to work on their assignments.
- Focus: PLCs can be used to solve any problem on campus. We have run them for the housing department, and we once helped our College of Education use a PLC to transfer a national journal. Despite Cox's desire to center on teaching and learning, we've found a better focus is scholarship. Almost every PLC we do begins with an academic text. For instance, we so loved John Medina's *Brain Rules* (2010) that we developed a PLC around it. When we facilitated our creativity PLC, we chose Erica McWilliam's *The Creative Workforce* (2008) and Daniel Pink's *A Whole New Mind* (2005). Sometimes no relevant book exists, so, for example, when we started a PLC on metacognition, we actually had to research the subject and provide the participants with a notebook of found scholarship.
- End Product: Traditionally we have linked PLCs to scholarship. Members are encouraged to create a publication out of their PLC product. For instance, last year we ran a PLC on flipping the classroom wherein we asked participants to submit articles for a book we were writing for New Forums, *It Works For Me, Flipping the Classroom* (2015). Another time our creativity PLC presented at a plenary session of a state conference.

- Dissemination: Books and conferences aren't the only way to publicize the work of a PLC. For our common core PLC, we not only provided syllabi in nine separate areas (e.g., English, physics, and communications), but published an article about a specific form of the learning community, the Embedded Professional Learning Community, that we invented to study the problem and implement a solution.

Subjects

How do we choose a subject worthy of a PLC? Sometimes an administrator or faculty member comes to us with a book, such as Derek Bok's *Our Underachieving Colleges* (2006) and even volunteers to facilitate. Reading the *Chronicle of Higher Education*, the *Wall Street Journal*, or even a popular magazine, we run across a book that seems promising, and we purchase a copy. Over the years we average reading twenty such books a year—*Borrowing Brilliance* (2009), *Blink* (2008), *Smart World* (2007) *Switch* (2007), *Academically Adrift* (2011)—and decide their application to our faculty is important. Sometimes the provost invites a speaker for her Professional Development Series, and so that the speaker's presentation doesn't become a forgotten one-shot, we continue its relevance through a PLC. This semester, for example, the provost has invited metacognition expert Saundra McGuire to campus, and so we will have either a spring or a next fall PLC based on her book. We also have a group of pedagogical ambassadors on campus we call the Faculty Innovators. Each summer we hold a retreat (we call it a "progress"), and one of the topics discussed is always future PLCs. This semester, for instance, one of our innovators last summer was fascinated with Mindset, Stereotyping, and Grit—guess what he's facilitating a PLC on this semester?

Next time we'll examine other aspects of PLCs.

Tips for Implementation

A. Identify significant problems/issues across campus that you and others (e.g., advisory board, your boss) deem worthy of further investigation. These issues can be scholarly, pedagogical, technical, or administrative.

B. Work to bring together individuals who share interest in the problem/concept/issue. We've found that constituting a PLC from a variety of disciplines brings broader perspectives and offers a bonus of building collaborations that probably wouldn't exist otherwise.

C. Set firm standards for attendance and participation. Faculty and professional staff are busy, and missing sessions or shirking responsibilities pose constant problems.

D. Require product. Never let a PLC devolve into a chat group. Be sure members realize that they are expected to produce something from their efforts, be it a publication, presentation, written plan, or white papers. PLCs' products contribute to the larger academic conversation.

E. Choose an effective facilitator. None of the first four tips matters if your facilitator is not trained (your job) and not effective.

Discussion Questions

A. Are you aware of certain problems or issues on campus that could use the attention of a group focused on answers/solutions?

B. Do you have a mechanism for identifying individuals interested in certain areas of concern? What incentives are available to bring interested but busy individuals to the table past their innate interests?

C. Do you have a way to identify prospective facilitators? Do you have a program (perhaps online) for training them in best practices? Can you offer incentives? (we've found the best facilitators come out of PLC membership).

D. Does your CTL have adequate funding to sponsor a PLC, given the attendant costs such as books, food, and perhaps even travel? Should/could you offer more than one during a semester?

Activities

A. Survey faculty, professional staff, and administrators to identify current problems/issues/interests that might call for a PLC.

B. Build a library of books and articles on current scholarly and pedagogical topics that might serve to whet the appetites of faculty and professional staff toward creating a PLC.

3. How to Assess Professional Learning Communities

(Posted 9 December 2015)

http://newforums.com/how-to-assess-professional-learning-communities/

In the beginning of our tenure as directors of the Teaching & Learning Center, we were happy just to find facilitators for our Professional Learning Communities (PLCs) and happier still when faculty and administrators signed up for them. Then reality set in. Most PLCs would finish with approximately half of those who originally signed up, and our cost (food, books, travel) didn't seem entirely justified by what we were getting out of them.

That's when we asked the question: what ARE we getting out of our PLCs? Numerically, we discovered that if we sponsored three PLCs per semester, every academic year we reached approximately 10% of our faculty (our programming reached 10% also, but some of those were also PLC participants). In the beginning—Phase I—we had some really effective PLC products. Our creativity PLC, for instance, presented a plenary session at the annual state-sponsored conference on teaching and learning. That same PLC also spun off a minor in Applied Creative Thinking as well as a series of books for New Forums (e.g., *Introduction to Applied Creative Thinking [2012]*). The PLC we ran of Senate Bill 1 and seamless transitioning Common Core-raised students into higher education produced a highly effective piece of intellectual property, the Embedded PLC. And the last two years we have run a PLC on metacognition that is helping us create a book for New Forums, *It Works For Me, Metacognitively*, as well as a repository for informative and instructional videos we call the Faculty Innovation Network (FIN).

But what was the effect of the PLC on the individual participants? For Phase II we decided to be creative and administer a survey of participants, the Enhanced Professional Learning Community Evaluation Form. We created a five-point Likert Scale (ranging from "Strongly Agree" to "Strongly Disagree") and asked each participant to rate seven statements:

1. I learned much from the scholarly component of my community.
2. I have a greater appreciation of the Scholarship of Teaching & Learning (SOTL) and am more willing to try it on my own.
3. I developed a real sense of community with my colleagues.
4. I have a greater sense of what my colleagues are trying to accomplish in their courses.
5. I will be able to use some things from this community in setting up my course goals andobjectives, teaching strategies, and course assessment methods.
6. This community was well-facilitated.
7. I find myself more willing to try to create a student learning community within a course I teach.

In addition, we asked participants what they found most helpful and to suggest what could be improved/revised.

As our PLCs evolved, so too did our assessment of them. Now, as we enter Phase III, we find ourselves once again revising our evaluation form. Our main reason is that we want to reduce the form to its most fundamental and powerful concepts, and in so doing we have decided to focus on what we consider the main impact of the PLC, learning and application. So far, we have three basic questions:

1. What do you consider the most important thing you learned from the PLC?
2. How did you apply that insight to your teaching?
3. Have you seen a positive change in student learning based on that application?

Sure, the earlier questions about facilitation and sense of community are important, but less so.

The major thing we have learned from our experience with PLCs is that faculty are very busy. At a teaching-centered institution of higher learning that has a 4-4 load as average, faculty, especially the non-tenured ones who must demonstrate proficiency in teaching, scholarship, and service, want simpler, less time-consuming professional development, even when they are fascinated by the PLC. And since we try to obtain a 100% response rate to our PLC evaluations, the shorter we can make them, the more likely faculty are to respond. More importantly, as the assessment movement gains greater and greater traction, the most important thing on which we can focus is still student learning. No matter what we do in a PLC, if it doesn't contribute to enhanced student learning, then we have not been effective.

After all, our unit's motto is "Helping teachers help students learn deeply."

Tips for Implementation

A. Determine your primary goal for PLCs you sponsor.

B. Develop a method for transmitting this goal to perspective PLC members.

C. Determine the simplest, most effective way to figure out if that goal is being met by PLC members.

Discussion Questions

A. How pedagogically oriented should a PLC be?

B. What percentage of achievement of a PLC's goal constitutes success?

C. Is the outlay of money, time, and resources justified for an initiative that impacts so few in its early stages? Could these things be more wisely invested in initiatives pointed toward greater numbers?

D. How important is it to you that a PLC develop a product?

Activities

A. Design an assessment tool for your PLCs that is both simple and effective in evaluating your goal(s).

B. Survey members of previous PLCs to determine the impact on members and the students they teach.

4. The Great Professional Learning Community Experiment

(Posted 27 January 2016)

http://newforums.com/professional-learning-community-experiment/

Everything can be innovated—case in point, the PLC.

While we have been using Professional Learning Communities (PLCs) on campus for the past decade (for more thorough information go to http://tlc.eku.edu/professional-learning-communities), we have always tried to **innovate** their use. Ten years ago Milton Cox, the godfather of PLCs, came to our campus to put on a workshop that introduced us to the traditional structure of PLCs, something we have written about in the past. What we saw, however, was not a fixed structure (e.g., 8-12 faculty study a subject for an entire semester and develop some enduring product), but an entity that we could repurpose for our various uses.

One semester, for instance, we emphasized **large numbers**, running approximately twenty PLCs in just the College of Education for everything from curriculum reform to transferring ownership of a state-run journal. In 2009 when the state decreed through Senate Bill

1 that we had to provide a seamless transition of common core standards from K-12 through postsecondary education, we created something we called the **Embedded PLC** wherein we facilitated a core PLC of ten members and then each one of the members facilitated a PLC in his/her respective areas (e.g., math, English, natural sciences, teacher preparation).

The Great PLC Experiment

This semester we tried another tweak—what we called the **Great PLC Experiment**. For the past decade every PLC we have run has had a minimal lifespan of an entire semester. Some PLCs are so popular that members, not wanting to see a good thing end, decide to continue through the next semester (e.g., flipping the classroom, metacognition, and cultural competency). We have seen the same continuation phenomenon in our Breakfast & a Book Series as our Sheryl Sandberg *Lean In* group continued for three consecutive semesters.

Like a lot of innovation, the PLC experiment derived from a problem. Last summer Tim, our cultural competency facilitator and Faculty Innovator, came to us with a dilemma. He wanted to continue all the work he had been doing with us, but as he also served as co-ordinator of the campus African African-American Studies program, he had responsibilities, especially in observation of his program's instructors, that needed to take place starting in mid-October.

Since every problem begs for a solution, we met with Tim and decided to try something new, what we now call the Compressed PLC. Basically, since by our definition a PLC must meet a minimum of eight times, we decided that the cultural competency PLC would hold meetings in each of the first eight weeks of the semester—our version of the new favorite in academic circles, the eight-week course. Having never tried this form of PLC, we knew a lot of **risk** was involved. Usually, an every-other-week meeting is preferred so that faculty don't feel overloaded by the add-on that is the PLC. Giving them more time helps ensure that members come to PLC meetings prepared.

Well, the semester is now over, and the PLC evaluations are in. While we feared members might complain about not having sufficient time to prepare excellent presentations, they revealed the opposite. Compression meant deeper engagement in the subject. Weekly meetings also reaped another benefit that put the "C" back in PLCs—deeper friendships. Meeting more often seemed to foster a greater sense of togetherness and shared purpose. Yes, we found a downside. Every PLC needs a product, and in this case we were developing a video repository as well as a book on cultural competency for New Forums Press. Eight weeks of study and presentations, however, left little time to develop the products.

What's the solution? Continue the PLC for another semester as we have in the past? Unfortunately, that solution puts a lot of pressure on the already overloaded facilitator. We have decided simply to work outside the PLC. Members can get help from Tim or the three of us on their writing and video development.

Had we not also been developing a minor in Applied Creative Thinking (ACT) and writing two books for New Forums—*Introduction to Applied Creative Thinking* (2012) and *Teaching Applied Creative Thinking* (2013)—while implementing a PLC program for campus, we might not have been so innovative. Certainly, our work with ACT led us to look at our successful programs from new perspectives and be open to taking risks where new opportunities presented themselves.

After all, innovation is a frame of mind that can be applied to any number of projects.

Tips for Implementation

A. Determine the success of current PLCs in terms of participant satisfaction and results (products and teaching innovations).

B. Consult with both facilitators and participants to assess their ideas on potential alternative formats for PLCs in terms of size, breadth, and time frame.

C. Run a few potential alternatives by individuals you can trust to get the opinions on the feasibility of the new formats.

Discussion Questions

A. Are you satisfied with the current format of your PLCs?

B. Have you run into problems with PLCs in terms of scheduling, securing facilitators, and filling slots?

C. Have you had suggestions from colleagues about alternative formats for PLCs?

Activities

A. Create and administer a survey to identify both satisfaction with current PLC formats and possible alternatives.

B. Gather the focus group of previous PLC facilitators and participants to identify potential alternative formats for future PLCs.

5. The Higher Education Professional Learning Community Oversight

(Posted 24 February 2016)

http://newforums.com/the-higher-ed-professional-learning-community-oversight/

Over the past ten years we have averaged sponsoring two professional learning communities (PLCs) per semester. It wasn't until we organized the Faculty Innovators, however, that we began to consider the concept of oversight. After we select, and sometimes train a facilitator, we have traditionally not observed him/her. Why? We could say that we haven't thought about it, but the truth is that most of the PLCs have taken place in the faculty lounge outside our office, so we have been very privy to what's going on.

This semester, though, the PLCs are being run across the campus, and we have lost contact. Also, as we have tried to organize our recently launched Faculty Innovators (FI) program, we have become very much aware of accountability, of keeping records, and of assessment. So, just as we launched the FI program before we had it completely figured out, we have decided to develop some sort of oversight of the PLCs on the fly.

As a model for keeping track of PLCs, we used the faculty consultation process (our faculty mentoring program), especially the classroom observation portion. As for a procedure, we opted for asking PLC facilitators to invite us to join the group whenever we could, not as an outside observer but as a potential participant. When we perform classroom observations, we give the instructor being observed the choice of mentioning the class has a guest today, explaining why, or just ignoring the two-hundred-pound gorilla in the room. For PLCs, we wanted to be introduced to the group and allowed to participate.

The difference for us is that classroom observations are accomplished with students in the room, but in a PLC all participants hold faculty rank. Therefore, for a faculty member to be present and not participating might be deemed strange. Besides, we usually have an expertise in whatever subject the PLC is studying. Last week we decided to give our oversight program a trial run, especially since Rusty was one of those facilitating a PLC, this one on the Scholarship of Teaching and Learning (SOTL).

Intrepidly, we sat down in a Monday morning PLC (also on SOTL) without a rubric to anchor the process. In fact, developing a rubric was one of the purposes of this visitation. Obviously, the observation focused not on the PLC's subject matter (and, yes, we were emailed the PLC's study materials before the session), but the facilitator with the participants as a secondary goal. Immediately, we encountered an unforeseen problem.

Most PLCs use a graduate seminar as a model, and in many seminars the instructor turns the bulk of classes over to individual students to teach (haven't we all heard that the best way to see if you really understand a subject is to teach it?). So when Charlie plopped himself in the seat, he found out that a faculty member other than the facilitator was teaching that day's assigned readings. Charlie adjusted; after all, when a graduate student becomes instructor for a day, the job of the assigned teacher is make sure things go right—to bring up information and viewpoints being missed, to bring discussions that get off the tracks back on, and to keep order.

But how can a rubric be set up to address all such contingencies?

Undaunted, on Friday Charlie joined Rusty's PLC. Grandmother used to say that "Comparisons are odious," but in academia playing one PLC session off another helps develop the rubric. Rusty had also relinquished some of his authority to a fellow faculty member, but Rusty was also more of an interventionist than the facilitator of the first PLC. In fact, he was quite subtle in bringing the PLC back to the assigned chapter. PLC members, like effective facilitators, must learn to maintain control, though that control is best when not noticed.

As a result of this experience, we have been talking about some general guidelines that will eventually be part of a PLC rubric:
- Does the PLC facilitator maintain some measure of control of the session?
- Does the PLC facilitator start by contextualizing the session's main lesson, or, in Gerry Nosich's term, begin with the day's "fundamental and powerful concept(s)"?

- Does the PLC facilitator help the session facilitator through the rough spots, especially in trying to make all faculty members present actual participants?
- Does the PLC facilitator provide all session facilitators with some tips (something else we will have to develop)?
- Has the facilitator preplanned the session so that each session is based on some outside resource/homework/reading?

Our overall point is that had we tried to create a rubric before actually observing some PLC sessions, we would have been missed a lot. Sometimes you have to take the risk of making up things as you go.

Tips for Implementation

A. Determine how much control you wish to exert relative to the format and presentation of individual PLCs.

B. Determine what role you want for the PLC's facilitator in terms of authority, percentage of presentation time, and responsibility for participation.

C. Determine your expectations for participants' involvement in PLCs. How active should a PLC member be? Any parameters for attendance? Contribution?

Discussion Questions

A. What constitutes a successful PLC in your mind? Do your thoughts align with the research?

B. Do you have preferences for session formats? How rigid are they?

C. What steps would you take if a PLC facilitator or participant were not living up to responsibilities?

Activities

A. Create a training rubric for PLC facilitators, outlining responsibilities and expectations.

B. Create a rubric for PLC participants, covering expectations on attendance, participation, and development of product.

6. A Third Type of Community

(Posted 23 December 2015)

http://newforums.com/third-community-type-for-high-ed-faculty/

A few years ago a group of faculty came to us, and because we had taught creative writing for years, they asked us to facilitate a fiction-writing group. No, fiction wasn't something they could claim on their promotion and tenure documents, but it was something they had always wanted to try (why didn't they try enrolling in our novel-writing class, we wondered). We had never done such a community, but since it sounded creative, we agreed.

Just this week that group published its third collabo-written novel.

Definition

Recently, we have been examining the two major types of faculty groups sponsored by CTLs, the Breakfast and a Book (B&B) and the Professional Learning Community (PLC). Our novel-writing group represents a third type we simply call the Creative Community. The Creative Community (CC) is called into being usually by a narrow, single task rather than a desire to study a subject broadly. Unlike the B&B, it focuses on a product, not discussion. And while a PLC studies the background research both on the topic and areas surrounding it (e.g., metacognition), the Creative Community has little concern with the "big picture." Actually, a Creative Community seems more like an academic workgroup, an ad hoc unit designed for a specific project. Workgroups, however, are usually constituted to solve an institutional problem that cuts across the disciplines (e.g., a strategic plan, a diversity initiative). The Creative Community is essentially a writing group producing a specific document (e.g., an academic article or a piece of fiction).

Years ago, for instance, we ran a PLC designed to introduce assessment to the University. Along the way, we invited Peggy Maki, an assessment expert, to campus, to facilitate a week of workshops. In one of her sessions, she happened to mention she was editing a collection of essays on how universities were responding to the call for assessment. A subgroup of six of us in the assessment PLC started talking with her, wondering if she would like an article about this university's attempts to develop and assessment strategy. When she invited us to participate, we decided we had to meet more frequently than our PLC had been. We divided up the writing into various sections, came together weekly (the assessment PLC met bi-weekly), and produced a chapter for Maki's *Coming to Terms with Student Outcomes Assessment* (2010), "From Bereavement to Assessment: The Transformation of a Regional Comprehensive University."

The Creative Community can be formed by any department, but because it often necessitates skills from differing disciplines, its organization is often best facilitated by a CTL. When we wrote on assessment, we asked two faculty members who weren't in our original PLC to join us because we needed their specialties. One member, for instance, was the head of Institutional Effectiveness at the University, while another had just done an assessment study for the College of Education.

In another instance, the dean of the College of Education came to us because his unit had been given a state grant to facilitate a newly-passed state law, Senate Bill 1, that mandated a seamless transition of Common Core between K-12 and postsecondary institutions. The dean asked how we would organize such a cross-campus effort. We picked two faculty members with whom we had worked in the past, and after several meetings we came up with a working document and methodology that, interestingly, involved our creating a series of interlocking PLCs.

Creative Communities, then, can be employed to solve immediate problems. Our

Common Core CC led to the formation of another group, our assessment CC basically executed a one-shot article, while our creative writing CC has been on-going for the past four years. That community began as a way of evaluating each other's fiction (e.g., a mystery short story that someone wanted to submit to *Ellery Queen's Mystery Magazine*) and transformed itself into the whole group working on a single project.

Basically, the success of the CC has encouraged us to beget several more. We encouraged a member of the College of Justice and Safety to work with a faculty member from psychology—yes, we would consider a two-person team a CC. For New Forums, we started a three-person team to write the *Introduction to Applied Creative Thinking* (2012) and a four-person team to write both *Teaching Applied Creative Thinking* (2013) and *Achieving Excellence in Teaching* (2014).

Three types of communities exist out there—try them.

Tips for Implementation

A. The Creative Community is the most difficult to facilitate. Don't try to sponsor such a PLC without identifying an expert in the field.

B. Entry qualifications for a Creative Community differ from a normal PLC. Such PLCs can only accept people proficient in the field. For example, if you are running a short fiction PLC, don't invite someone who has never written short fiction before. In short, these types of PLCs are not entry level, 101 levels.

Discussion Questions

A. Boyer's *Scholarship Reconsidered* (1990) never listed the scholarship of creative endeavor as a fifth type, and many universities do not even recognize this area. Should they?

B. What constitutes proficiency in the arts vs. a scholarly/pedagogical PLC?

Activities

A. Construct a proficiency rubric for a potential Creative Community.

b. Determine what products would be acceptable for a Creative Community.

E. Implementing Innovative Pedagogical Strategies

1. A Reaction to Worthen's 'Lecture Me, Really'

(Posted 16 December 2015)

http://newforums.com/a-reaction-to-worthens-lecture-me-really/

Perhaps the reports of the death of the Sage-on-the-Stage are premature. Periodically defenders of the lecture approach to teaching rise up to be heard. Last week, for instance, continuing op-ed writer Molly Worthen produced "Lecture Me. Really," a pro-lecture piece aimed at preserving a traditional tool in humanities pedagogy for the *New York Times Sunday Review* (http://www.nytimes.com/2015/10/18/opinions/sunday/lecture-me-really.html?emc=etal&_r=0).

Worthen's defense centers on several factors:
- Active learning is a "craze" that partakes of "that other great American pastime, populist resentment of experts."
- Lectures are "essential for teaching the humanities most basic skills: comprehension and reasoning . . . the art of attention . . . the 'building of an argument' . . . ."
- Lectures are not always pure lectures and can include questioning.
- Lectures communicate "the emotional vitality of the intellectual endeavor."
- Students synthesize the lecture into notes.
- Students learn critical thinking.

Despite Worthen's insistence that "Today's vogue for active learning is nothing new," active learning as we know it came into the academy during the last decade of the Twentieth Century. Concerned with teaching, the lecture method primarily envisioned students as passive recipients of knowledge, while the key word in "active learning" is **learning**—focusing on what knowledge, skills, and values students gain in college courses. Twenty-five years with a growing reputation and body of research make active learning more than a "craze."

Problems with Lecturing

One major problem with the lecture method is that it does not accomplish what Worthen claims as one of its virtues: it does not lead to students developing attention spans. As we emphasized in our New Forums publication *Teaching Applied Creative Thinking* (2013), Penner (1984) states an hour-long lecture "outlasts a student's attention span by 40-50 minutes, so much of even a good lecture is lost. As Medina (2008) puts it, 'Before the last quarter-hour is over in a typical presentation, people usually have checked out'" (pp. 7-8). In fact, later in *Brain Rules* (2008) Medina pegs the average student attention span somewhere around 12 minutes. Not only do students check out, but, more importantly, they retain almost none of what they hear in a lecture.

Why don't students retain what they hear in lectures, even when they take notes? **Retrieval**. Moving information from one's short-term memory to one's long-term memory demands constant retrieval of the information. And retrieval happens in such active learning activities as group work and reflection. Instead of merely remembering or understanding, skills suggested by lecturing, students need to pull information from their memory and utilize it through one of the four revised Bloom's higher-order thinking skills—applying, analyzing, evaluating, and creating.

Do lectures promote critical thinking? As Jake Barnes says in Hemingway's *The Sun Also Rises* (1926), "Isn't it pretty to think so?" We ran across a study that claimed up until a few years ago 90% of all P-20 classes still relied primarily on the lecture method. According to Arum and Roksa's *Academically Adrift* (2011), which used CLAP tests as the basis for its analysis, half of all college graduates demonstrated no significant improvement in their critical thinking or writing skills during their higher education years. Students can't build arguments well or write them either.

Finally, the student's synthesizing the lecture into notes does not necessarily rely on the delivery of the information by lecture. More important is how the student studies. Brown, Roediger, and McDaniel's *Make It Stick* (2014) offers some good study habits to develop:
- Practice retrieving from memory vs. rereading the text or other instructional material—e.g., lecture.
- Space out the practice.
- Switch between topics (e.g., English and psychology).
- Make practice tests.
- Do rewrite by hand, not on your computer.

A Solution

Finally, let's stop looking at this issue in black and white terms—you must use either the lecture method or active learning. Why not try the **mini-lecture**? Information can still be provided in 12-minute chunks, especially if you follow some guidelines:
- <u>Lead</u> the mini-lecture with a relevant story that both interests the audience and illustrates a key point.
- <u>Focus</u> the mini-lecture on the most fundamental and powerful concepts of the session.
- Intersperse the lecture, as Worthen suggests, with questions aimed at provoking discussion, and don't ask for student participation—demand it.
- <u>Build</u> your active learning components of group work and written reflections out of your key mini-lecture points.
- <u>Structure</u> your pre or post-lecture instruction around the higher-order revised Bloom activities of applying, analyzing, evaluating, and creating.
- <u>Try to develop</u> a metacognitive awareness in your students of the best practices in effective learning.

Tips for Implementation

A. Read the latest research on teaching-learning strategies.

B. Survey your faculty to determine which teaching paradigm is preferred/practiced.

C. Plan a series of workshops to introduce alternatives to the straight lecture approach.

Discussion Questions

A. What is your preferred teaching paradigm? Can you defend it?

B. What is your attitude toward using a variety of approaches to classroom presentation?

C. What is your attitude on the effectiveness of the lecture? The mini-lecture?

Activities

A. Present a session to a group of faculty members using the lecture exclusively.

B. Present the same material to a second group using a variety of approaches, including the mini-lecture, active learning, and group work.

C. One week after the presentations, send out an electronic assessment of the material.

2. Flipping the Classroom, New Book in It Works for Me Series

(Posted 14 April 2015)

http://newforums.com/flipping-the-classroom-new-book-it-works-for-me-series/

Recently, New Forums published the eighth book in our *It Works for Me, Flipping the Classroom*(2015), and we couldn't be more excited. Way back in the last century, we began the series with *It Works for Me! Shared Tips for Teaching* (1998), what we thought of as a one-shot of practical tips. At the time only two of us served as editors (Rusty would join us with the most recent book), and we were primarily professors of English interested in helping our newer colleagues navigate the treacherous tidal waves of tenure, but, realizing we had a few more tips in us, we started issuing an average of a book every other year.

Along the way we began to realize how vast the area of pedagogy is, and we made a major career move, shifting from being mostly professors of creative writing to professional developers co-directing for the University's newly-created Teaching & Learning Center. We began to publish pieces in such professional forums as the *Journal of Faculty Development* and learned we were practicing what had become known as the Scholarship of Teaching and Learning (SOTL).

In *Enhancing Scholarly Work on Teaching & Learning* (2006), Maryellen Weimer posits that the field of SOTL is large, running the gamut from practitioner pedagogical scholarship to pure education research. In Weimer's terms we began our entry into SOTL with the former and moved toward the latter. Our early New Forums books focus mostly on specific experiential tips, but gradually evolved toward more specific domains such as scholarship, creativity, and now the bleeding edge with flipping the classroom. We've gotten more specific with a tribute book to our old field, creative writing with *Options* (2014), while at the same time we tried to sum up recent trends in higher ed research with *Achieving Excellence in Teaching* (2014).

If one theme other than practical pedagogy emerges in our writing, it's probably creativity. While we always stressed being a creative instructor, in the past four years we've focused on the growing discipline of creative thinking with *It Works for Me, Creatively* (2011), *Introduction to Applied Creative Thinking* (2012), and *Teaching Applied Creative Thinking* (2013). While our newest book on flipping the classroom doesn't focus on creativity per se, it did result from Bloom's higher-order thinking skills of applying and creating.

In *Introduction to Applied Creative Thinking* (2012), we present nine basic strategies of creative thinking, beginning with **perception shift**, which we say "involves looking at a person, idea, or situation from a new perspective" (p. 28). Flipping the classroom stands as an excellent example of practical perception shift. Educators began reflecting on such societal trends as the rise of active learning replacing the sage on the stage, the sudden spurt of technology (especially the Internet), and advances in brain science. One result was the experiment of "flipping" the two major portions of the learning experience, the classroom and "homework." In simple terms professors began providing what had been their usual classroom lectures along with traditional assignments as the homework portion and utilizing the more limited classroom time for higher-order (Bloom) activities that aided in students' deep learning.

It Works for Me, Flipping the Classroom (IWFMFTC) focuses on this paradigm shift. The book begins with some essays about transitioning into a flipped classroom, moves to a section on out-of-class assignments, and then lists some in-class activities for the flipper. After a section on electronic resources, the book ends with ever-important ways to assess the effectiveness of the flipped class. In short, IWFMFTC serves as a handbook for the would-be flipper, providing guidelines, exercises, and tips along the way.

Why should you try this book? Professional development means more than staying current in one's chosen discipline. The complete instructor needs a familiarity with current trends in higher education as well as advances in technology. ITWMFTC offers a quick introduction to that very crossroads. It's the kind of book Poe would have liked as it can be read in a single session, but it can also be the academic equivalent of power bars, providing energizing snacks at key moments.

Feast or munch—it's your choice.

Tips for Implementation

A. Pick one class that you enjoy teaching each semester but might need extra attention. Focus on flipping one or two modules or lessons from that class.

B. After deciding the course or lesson you will flip, establish parameters and methods for collecting data or assessing the flipped classroom approach. Ensure that you have established classes or dates to collect data or feedback about your flipped classes.

C. Pursue approaches or plans to share your experiences and data in your CTL programming and at conferences or publications. Establish your presentation goals up front.

Discussion Questions

A. How do your flipped courses or lessons compare to your traditional lessons or lectures?

B. How might you use your experience flipping your classroom to improve your own teaching, the teaching of others, or the programming in your CTL?

Activities

A. Establish a plan for flipping your classroom. The plan should include timeline/schedule, syllabus, lesson plan(s), research question(s).

B. List two or three Faculty Learning Outcomes (FLOs) (see Hurney, Brantmeier, Good, Harrison, & Meixner, 2016) that you expect to gain from this experience.

Section References

Blythe, H., Sweet, C., & Carpenter, R. (2015). *It works for me, flipping the classroom: Shared tips for effective teaching.* Stillwater, OK: New Forums.

Hurney, C. A., Brantmeier, E. J., Good, M. R., Harrison, D., & Meixner, C. (2016). The faculty learning outcome assessment framework. *Journal of Faculty Development 30*(2), 69-77.

3. Making It C.R.I.S.P.

(Posted 10 August 2016)

http://newforums.com/making-it-crisp-using-information-organization-and-retrieval-for-deep-learning/

In *Achieving Excellence in Teaching* (2014) we devote a chapter to the importance of organization in instruction, especially individual class organization. To help faculty teach, we have created C.R.I.S.P., "a classroom methodology based on unity of purpose as it organizing principle [that] involves five ordered and inter-related steps" (pp. 49-50):

- **Contextualize**: at the beginning announce the fundamental and powerful concepts around which the day's instruction will revolve.
- **Review**: tie the day's concept(s) to previously discussed ideas—i.e., students learn best when new knowledge is attached to old.
- **Iterate**: emphasize the key concept(s) several times throughout the class in a variety of ways.
- **Summarize**: at the end of class, stop in time to go over the key concept(s) whether through reminders, student recall, or reflection papers.

- **Preview**: when you assign the material for the next class, inform your students what they need to be looking for in the material.

Recently, we've been reading Brown, Roediger, and McDaniel's *Make It Stick* (Cambridge: Harvard UP, 2014)—not to be confused with a book we cite in *Achieving Excellence in Teaching*, the Heath's *Made to Stick* (2007)—whose subtitle encapsulates its premise: *The Science of Successful Learning*. What we found is a text chock full of learning techniques that supplement as well as reinforce C.R.I.S.P.

Written for both instructors and students, *Make It Stick* begins by debunking students' traditional learning strategies of rereading text and massed practice of a skill. Instead, to aid in learning fundamental and powerful concepts, the authors point to the research in cognitive psychology underlying **retrieval practice**, "recalling facts or concepts or events from memory" (p. 3). The more familiarity students gain from retrieving learning from memory, the closer they come to what we consider the goal of higher education, **deep learning**, or learning that endures, even changing one's mental model of the world. According to *Make It Stick*, retrieval practice has two profound benefits:

- "One, it tells you what you know and don't know, and therefore where to focus further study to improve the areas where you're weak."
- "Two, recalling what you have learned causes your brain to reconsolidate the memory, which strengthens its connections to what you know and makes it easier for you to recall in the future" (p. 20).

Practicing retrieval, the authors conclude, "makes learning stick far better than reexposure to the original material does" (p. 28).

To iterate and summarize, Brown, Roediger, and McDaniel suggest several methods for the student and instructor:

- **Flashcards** (they both strengthen the memory and interrupt forgetting)
- **Quizzing** (after reading or at the end of class). We have always advocated giving a daily quiz that is part of the student's grade (around 20%) so something is at stake.
- **Reflection.** In *Achieving Excellence in Teaching*, we cover this concept under "Summarize" p. (52).
- **Elaboration,** the "process of giving new material meaning by expressing it in your own words and connecting it with what you know "(5), something we discuss under "Iterate" (p. 51).
- **Putting new knowledge into a larger context** (see our "Contextualize"). In addition, the authors add several refinements to the retrieval strategy:
- **Spacing**—rather than one large cram session, use multiple sessions so that some forgetting has taken place. For the teacher, this method means that every reference to a key concept is not contained in one five-minute block; instead, periodically return to the crux of the session.

- **Feedback**—immediately after a quiz, go over the correct answer. Flashcards work on the same principle because when they are turned over, the user can tell whether the correct version was given (for that matter, always speak out loud when employing flashcards so that the user can't simply say, "I knew that." Our buddy Dee Fink, author of *Creating Significant Learning Experiences* (2003), offers a modern alternative to the traditional flashcard with the scratch-off forms that like scratch-off lottery cards provide immediate confirmation or denial of one's answer.
- **Interleaving**—although it sounds counterintuitive, practice retrieval with two or more subjects. The gains will be slower at first, but what you learn will last longer.
- **Varied practice**—practice at different times, in different places, and with flashcards use different orders.

Our C.R.I.S.P., then, becomes even more effective as a class organizing methodology when instructors create questions, quizzes, and written reflections that call on the student to constantly retrieve information.

Tips for Implementation

A. Try both C.R.I.S.P. and *Make It Stick* in class.

B. As research comes out daily on retention and deep learning, start scanning the journals for it. Don't be afraid to go out of your field. We don't fully understand neuroscience either, but we can read an abstract.

Discussion Questions

A. Why do you think so little research into retention was performed until recently? Why, then, when science started producing results was academia slow to implement the research?

B. Is good teaching an art, a science, or both?

Activities

A. Follow up on Tip A. Run a comparison study of the two methods. Some people aren't convinced by the research evidence, but rather by the personal experience.

B. Apply C.R.I.S.P. and the *Make It Stick* principles to one specific class you will be teaching this semester. In the period after the applied teaching and learning experiment, rather than a formal survey, hold an informal discussion with your class about the pros and cons.

4. Applying C.R.I.S.P. to Change Higher Education Campus Culture

(Posted 11 May 2016)

http://newforums.com/four-rs-deep-learning/

In chapter nine of our *Achieving Excellence in Teaching* (2014), we explain the importance of using CRISP* as an organizational principle for effective classroom instruction in order to help students learn deeply. As we say there, "CRISP is an acronym for classroom methodology based on unity of purpose as an organizational principle; the process involves five ordered and inter-related steps: Contextualize, Review, Iterate, Summarize, and Preview" (pp. 54-55).

Recently, we have also discovered that the same five-step process of organization that promotes deep learning in the classroom can be effectively applied to other campus initiatives to bring about deep learning in stakeholders. In short, by applying CRISP to these initiatives, we feel we have contributed to changing the campus climate.

Example One. As Co-Directors of the Teaching & Learning Center (TLC), Hal and Charlie were often asked, "What do you guys do over there anyway?" Relying on our CRISP principle, we knew we had to come up with a **context**, a succinct fundamental and powerful concept that both encapsulated our mission and was easily remembered. Our first response showed up on our website as our motto, "Helping Teachers Help Students Learn." Then, when we sat down to write *Achieving Excellence in Teaching*, (2014), we asked ourselves not only what were the major characteristics of a terrific teacher, but what was the end purpose of all these strategies? Life-long proponents of Roethke's "I learn by going where I have to go," we centered the book's chapter three on our answer—the key reason for these strategies, deep learning. That insight caused us to make a subtle change in our TLC motto to "Helping Teachers Help Students Learn Deeply."

Example Two. As all three of us facilitate our institution's New Faculty Orientation (NFO), we realized that we were providing five days of orientation that went in a dozen directions: campus ID, campus tour, tour of the 22-county service region, getting a laptop, meeting with chairs and deans, talking with HR about benefits, etc. But what was our focus? When we tried to be all things to new faculty, we found our message was dispersed in many ways, and like a lecture that's all over the place, we wondered what the new faculty was learning. Did they have a dominant take-away from NFO? Taking a cue from our motto, we knew we had to once again **contextualize**. After brainstorming on what should be our key concept, we came up with another succinct statement: "Excellence in Teaching Is Job One." With that statement as our guiding light, we reduced New Faculty Orientation to three days and, more importantly, achieved our context. We now begin on a Wednesday with a morning consisting of two workshops: one on Best Pedagogical Practices (which we not only talk about but demonstrate) and another on What We Teach. As a result, our NFO evaluations have gone through the roof as the new faculty received a concentrated message on the importance our institution places on good teaching. Moreover, we've taken a suggestion from our Operations Specialist, and at the bottom of all campus emails we send we broadcast the fundamental and powerful concept that "Excellence in Teaching Is Job One."

Example Three. When we finally convinced the provost that our institution needed a Faculty Excellence in Teaching Program (FETP), one of the reasons we were able to accomplish this task was the constant **iteration** through saturation in our emails, presentations, and workshops of our previous two fundamental and powerful ideas. Our FETP provided an application of the two ideas and used **review** to tie to them (new knowledge is built upon old).

In **summary**, our point is simple. Whether as a teacher or as part of a larger unit, if you want to get your message across for some future endeavor—**preview**—try to be CRISP about it.

References

*This post is based on: Blythe, H. & Sweet, C. (2008). "Keeping You Class C.R.I.S.P." *NEA Higher Education Advocate* 26 (2): 5-8. Print.

Tips for Implementation

A. Determine the central goal of your faculty development program.

B. Determine ways in which this goal can impact other programs and initiatives across campus.

C. Determine ways in which you can gain collaboration with these programs and initiatives.

Discussion Questions

A. Do you think the C.R.I.S.P. approach is a valid organizational principle?

B. What problems do you see with C.R.I.S.P. as an organizational principle?

Activities

A. Pick a campus initiative and determine if the C.R.I.S.P. approach could make it more effective.

B. Brainstorm ways in which C.R.I.S.P. could be used on your campus with trusted colleagues.

5. The Four Rs of Deep Learning

(Posted 30 December 2014)

http://newforums.com/four-rs-deep-learning/

Have you discovered like us that when you go to professional conferences, the most enjoyable and productive moments occur when you are sitting down informally with friends discussing old memories and new developments in the field? It's that time of year when faculty are not only winding down the fall semester, but already gearing up for the spring. While spending last weekend at the 34th annual Lilly International Conference on College Teaching, we gained an insight into some concepts that will help you prepare your syllabi.

Early Friday morning we found ourselves seated at a table with old friends Dee Fink, who wrote the seminal *Creating Significant Learning Experiences* (2003), and Greg Wentzell, the Conference's assistant director. After a lively discussion of our diets and health habits, we segued into a debate on the essentials of a good class. Now we're big believers that 90-95% of syllabus preparation for the majority of professors is content, not pedagogy. Why? Because most disciplines train their students to think of the field first and the instruction second, if at all. So, accepting Gerry Nosich's theory on focusing a class on fundamental and powerful concepts, and trying to simplify things for professors only recently starting to be concerned about student learning, we posed a question: what is the minimal amount of significant pedagogical material that a professor needs to include in each class?

We started by agreeing on the goal of college instruction—in our *Achieving Excellence in Teaching; A Self-help Guide* (2014) we proclaimed it **deep learning**, while Dee likes the phrase "significant learning experiences" and someone else voted for "life-long learning." We then proceeded to Dee's sequence of activities for the whole course, and after adding in some material we had gleaned from *Make It Stick* (2014)—a book we have discussed in previous posts—we jotted down on the back of a conference flyer something we now call the four foundations of deep learning—the four R's of higher education.

First, students must **receive information**. Here the instructor—no matter whether the basic methodology is lecture, discussion, small group work, or watching a video—dispenses contextualized data (printed or online) for the student's consumption. This information will be added to the student's old knowledge to construct new knowledge.

Second, students must **retrieve information** through practice in order to move it into their long-term memory. In-class activities such as discussion, whether teacher-student or student-student, provide one method for retrieval. Daily tests at the beginning and end of class likewise necessitate retrieval. Short and long papers in and out of class offer an opportunity to apply that new information. The more frequent the retrieval opportunities the instructor delivers, the greater the chances for deep learning.

Third, students must **rate** the information through meaningful and fairly immediate feedback. Developing student critical learning skills is important, for critical thinking is essentially the evaluation of argument and information, but students also need the instructor's aid. Sometimes that feedback is verbal (such as in class discussion), sometimes it's the grade on the paper or test/exam/quiz (as well as the instructor going over the correct answers), and sometimes it's an email response to a student question, but it has to be as immediate as possible.

Finally, students must **reflect** on that information. Students need to become metacognitive, monitoring their learning process, and that process must be stimulated. Mid-class and end-of-class reflections on a daily basis help build that understanding. An effective end-of-class assessment asks students to reflect upon not only what they learned, but what ways they found worked best to achieve knowledge.

When we started our grade-school education, its basis in learning was the three Rs—reading, writing, and 'rithmetic. Now the four Rs of receiving, retrieving, rating, and reflecting provide a solid foundation for higher education. When you begin making your syllabus for next semester, don't just worry about what you will be teaching—emphasize the how in each class session, and you'll be starting students down the path of deep learning.

Tips for Implementing

A. Determine what approaches to teaching prevail on your campus.

B. Determine both the understanding of and the desire for deep learning on your campus.

C. Become acquainted with the latest research on deep learning, including higher-order thinking skills, retrieval techniques, and metacognition-reflection.

Discussion Questions

A. How important do you believe teaching for deep learning is?
B. Do you think the four Four-R approach to deep learning is valid? Workable?
C. Do you find any weaknesses in the Four-R approach? Possible adjustments?

Activities

A. Present an active learning workshop on the Four-R approach to deep learning.
B. Survey your campus for ideas on achieving deep learning.

6. The Importance of Physical Space for Faculty Performance

(Posted 1 June 2016)

http://newforums.com/the-importance-of-physical-space-for-faculty-performance/

While space was the final frontier for countless episodes of *Star Trek*, creating the optimal teaching and learning spaces may be the final academic frontier for Centers of Teaching and Learning (CTLs). As Tom Kelley, CEO of IDEO put it in his "Forward" to *Make Space*

(2012), "Space matters. We read our physical environment like we read a human face" (p. 4).

The importance of physical space is a concept we delved into in both *Teaching Applied Creative Thinking* (2013)—see Chapter V on "The Learning Environment for Optimal Creative Thinking"—and *Transforming Your Students into Deep Learners* (2016)—see "Strategy VII: Creating Spaces for Deep Learning." In these books, we enunciated several key principles for achieving Kelley's goal: "Space is a valuable tool that can help you create deep and meaningful collaborations in your work and life" (p. 5).

At the moment, our CTL includes three major spaces: the Noel Studio for Academic Creativity (a space housed in the campus library with a large open area, a high-tech classroom, breakout spaces for small-group collaboration, presentation practice rooms, and a media wall with large monitors), the Teaching & Learning Center (consisting of two offices and a 33x37 foot Faculty Lounge), and a new space in the old campus bowling alley for us to build an experimental classroom. The Noel Studio was completed in 2010, and the Faculty lounge in 1939.

Rebuilding a Space by Principles

This past year, we have been refurbishing the 75+-year-old Faculty Lounge, an Art Deco relic of opulence. Forty years ago the Faculty Lounge was the campus version of the 18th-century coffee house. Faculty came from across campus and often had to wait for a seat. In an era before social media and campus email, the lounge was where one learned what was happening on campus, official and unofficially (the rumor mill ran as often at the coffee grinder). Our central focus in the refurb was to transform the space from a comfortable lounge of yesteryear to a trendy, contemporary workshop space that invited faculty in to participate.

Our first upgrade was obviously technological. We had a new wireless access point installed that could handle heavy traffic. From that time we met quite often and followed several design principles we brought out in *Teaching Applied Creative Thinking* (2013):

- **Natural light**
- **Bright colors**
- **Flexible and comfortable furniture**
- **Writable spaces** (pp. 23-24).

The Faculty Lounge has two large east-facing windows as well as a French door, so we have plenty of natural light (in fact, so much light beams through in the early morning that shades are a must). Overhead lighting consists of four decorative but dim lights as well as a light circle we refer to as the Cone of Silence (thank you, *Get Smart*). Given the building's basic knob-and-tube wiring system (our budget prohibits such extensive rewiring), the most effective upgrade was switching to LED lights.

Bright colors (which adorn the Noel Studio) presented a problem for the Faculty Lounge. The space is fairly traditional. As a result, we have lighter colors on the walls and even some colorful paintings and posters. The rug is basically a multi-colored brown, the tables are a dark wood, and the chairs contain a mixture of blues and grays. Obviously, combining the past and present necessitated a compromise.

Aside from the colors, the furniture's main element is movability. We have seven tables with six chairs, and all seven tables can be reconfigured to achieve Kelley's "deep and meaningful collaborations." As the lounge contains a fireplace, we built a foundation of a sofa and two chairs in front of it. In its previous iteration, the lounge contained eight wheelless, square tables, each able to seat only four people. As a result of the upgraded space, we will now be able to accommodate 50 people for interactive faculty development sessions.

Writable spaces also followed the principle of movability. Rather than try to attach screens to old plaster-and-lath walls, we went with two smartboards and two monitors on wheels. The latter meant that even for presentations we wouldn't need the traditional projector and screen because anyone can access the movable monitors.

The Key Principle: Mentoring from the Middle

Our major principle was not spatial, but pedagogical. In *Teaching Applied Creative Thinking* (2013) we stressed the importance of spatial and technological decisions emanating from pedagogical preferences, and in the same book we posited that the teaching and learning paradigm best suited for students is the **Mentor from the Middle**. Obviously, such a pedagogical concept underscores the need for the instructor/mentor not to be a sage at the front of the room or even a guide on its side, but rather a teacher-learner immersed in the middle of the group. To translate this concept into reality necessitated running a thin, flat wire under the rug to a podium/pocket cart at its center.

Conclusion

The new workshop space debuts this fall. We plan to run all our Teaching & Learning Innovation (TLI) series workshops in it as well as our three-to-four Professional Learning Communities. More importantly, we plan to assess how the faculty interacts in this new space, including how it is used and how it functions and whether their collaborations actually result in deep learning.

To paraphrase Wittgenstein, the limits of my space mean the limits of my world. The more optimal the space, the more optimal the learning.

Tips for Implementation

A. Coordinate learning space planning with key stakeholders from representative disciplines, departments, or colleges at your institution.

B. Design rubrics to discuss and determine the components and features of the space you need to design (include a link to RC's TLC space design template).

C. Explore spatial zones (see Bunnell, Carpenter, Hensley, Williams, & Winter, 2016) and your priorities for the space. A priority for the Noel Studio for Academic Creativity space, for example, was creating visually inscribable spaces (Carpenter, 2014).

Discussion Questions

A. What are the priorities for your learning space(s)? Create a list of priorities, including the teaching and learning activities you expect to take place. Once you've created your initial list, scale these activities to technologies and furniture that you would like to enhance the space.

B. Discuss teaching and learning priorities with colleagues at your institution. What ideas or concerns do they have?

C. What spaces are currently used for faculty development at your institution? How might these spaces be enhanced to engage all faculty as learners?

Activities

A. Create an inventory listing ways in which these learning spaces will be used. Who is the audience? Are they intended as classroom spaces with student activity, faculty spaces, or mixed use?

B. Create a learning space design rubric to share with colleagues and gather input from key stakeholders or faculty from across disciplines. You can use or adapt this teaching and learning space rubric (link to RC's for the TLC).

Section References

Bunnell, Adam, Russell Carpenter, Emily Hensley, Kelsey Strong, ReBecca Williams, and Rachel Winter. (2016). "Mapping the Hot Spots: A Zoning Approach to Space Analysis and Design." *Journal of Learning Spaces,* 5(1), 19-25.

Carpenter, Russell. (2014). "Negotiating the Spaces of Design in Multimodal Composition." *Computers and Composition: An International Journal, 33*(1), 68-78.

Doorley, Scott, and Witthoft, Scott. (2011). *Make space: How to set the stage for creative collaboration.* Malden, MA: Wiley.

7. 7 Tips for Making the Most of Higher Ed Instructional Videos

(Posted 21 October 2014)

http://newforums.com/making-instructional-videos/

Recently we have been involved with a Professional Learning Community on Flipping the Classroom as well as creating our Teacher's Toolbox, an on-demand professional development website where faculty can access informative videos on a range of subjects. In both cases, a key component is the instructional video, so we have been working on guidelines for effective videos whether they are aimed at faculty or students.

1. <u>Have the goal of producing deep learning.</u> In our *Achieving Excellence in Teaching*

(2014), we state, "Deep Learners build new knowledge on previous knowledge (a process that is accelerated when the learner cares about the subject under consideration), critically analyze the new knowledge, and, because of the new knowledge, even change their mental model of reality" (p. 15). You want your video to stick in the mind of your audience and hopefully alter that mind's way of perceiving the world.

2. <u>Keep it brief</u>. Just as mini-lectures in class lose their audience after about ten minutes, so the attention of the video audience will fall off at just about the same rate. Shoot for the ten-minute limit, and try not to go much over it.

3. <u>Tell a story</u>. Right now we're shooting a video about the demographics of the typical EKU student. It starts at a first-year dorm and ends in the place where graduation is held. In other words, we are replicating the typical journey of an EKU student. We have experience writing film and TV scripts, but all you need is a rough outline.

4. <u>Focus on fundamental and powerful concepts</u>. In ten minutes you can't produce a documentary or even a short-short, but you don't want to. As Gerry Nosich points out in *Learning To Think Things Through* (Upper Saddle River: Pearson, 2009), "A fundamental and powerful concept is one that can be used to explain or think out a huge body of questions, problems, information, and situations" (p. 105). Obviously, when we researched the EKU student demographics, we came across reams of data, but we distilled that information down to the most basic details that relate to our students' ability to learn.

5. <u>Emphasize the visual quality</u>. Of course, in a video this guideline sounds obvious, but too many videos look like a painter's capturing of still life. In *Brain Rules* (Seattle: Pear Press, 2008), John Medina says, "Put simply, the more visual the input becomes, the more likely it is to be recognized—and recalled . . . . If information is presented orally, people remember about 10%, tested 72 hours after exposure. That figure goes up to 65% if you add a picture" (pp. 233-4). Add charts, maps, short videos, and images to your videos to engage your audience.

6. <u>Use interesting angles</u>. A ten-minute video of you sitting at your desk intoning about the Boer Wars is a poor substitute for a map, a short movie clip, and some actual pics. Our ancestors, the reason you are here today, walked an average of 12 miles a day learning to survive. This motion, even if a different angle, may be the key to your audience surviving to the end of your video.

7. <u>Try for good, if not professional quality</u>. Simple software like Avid, Adobe Premier Elements, iMovie, Camtasia Studio, or Moviemaker will help. So will practice. Most of us have not spent a few semesters in film school, but watching someone else's videos will help.

Tips for Implementation

A. Determine your program's capacity for producing instructional videos.
B. Determine what subjects for videos take precedence.
C. Determine the best software for developing the videos you desire.

Discussion Questions

A. How important do you think instructional video is to your faculty development program?

B. Do you believe instructional video is worth the cost of start-up, maintenance, and updating?

C. Do you think you can co-ordinate production of instructional videos with other campus units necessary?

Activities

A. Assemble a team to produce a trial video on a faculty development topic you have ascertained as important.

B. Sponsor a competition to produce an effective script for an instructional video.

F. Promoting Scholarship

1. Kentucky Pedagogicon: How We Did It

(Posted 17 August 2016)

http://newforums.com/kentucky-pedagogicon-how-we-did-it/

For the past few years we have argued that the traditional three-part list of faculty responsibilities—teaching, scholarship, and service—needs to be a tetrad. Underlying the traditional trio should be professional development, and to push PD, the past two years we have facilitated a state-wide PD conference for higher education instructors that we call the Kentucky Pedagogicon.

Higher education in Kentucky is overseen by the Council on Postsecondary Education (CPE), and years ago it created the Faculty Development Workgroup, whose purpose was to provide Kentucky's college and universities (private and public, two-year and four-year) with PD guidance. Some years ago the PD and IT groups merged their annual conferences, but the result soon became more IT and less PD.

The FDW, of which we are a member, decided to start over by separating the groups into two conferences. In our way of thinking the old Chinese proverb that "The beginning of wisdom is learning to call things by their right name" took on new importance. The merged conference had been called the Kentucky Convergence Conference, a name that meant little. Taking our cue from a group whose name immediately announces their audience, the [insert city] Comicon, we decided to relaunch the annual meeting as the Kentucky Pedagogicon. Yes, the name called attention to itself, but it left no doubt that the emphasis would be on teaching and learning.

Next, as Kentucky is large, taking eight hours to make the southwest to northeast corner drive from Paducah to Ashland, we volunteered to hold the conference in Richmond as Eastern Kentucky University, despite its geographical name, sits close to the commonwealth's center. We also decided that to save money, we would condense the conference to a single day. That way, even attendees from our far corners would have to foot the bill for only one night's stay. Running the conference from (9:00-4:00 also made it possible for folks to attend the day-long conference and still make it home that night.

When to hold the conference was another key choice. The school year was busy enough, and we knew faculty wanted their summers for research and travel, so we picked the Friday after most state graduations. While no time was perfect, the Pedagogicon was held right after faculty turned in their spring semester grades and before they departed for the summer.

Every June the CPE Faculty Development Workgroup holds a retreat, so we used the retreat to plan the conference theme (e.g., Closing the Achievement Gap , Practicing Creative and Scholarly Teaching) and establish a schedule. The Call For Proposals goes out on 1 November, and a committee of the FDW meets in mid-February to select 30+ proposals (six rounds with six sessions each round-sponsors' sessions) plus posters (participants are given box lunches and encouraged to interact with the poster creators). One of our reps serves as a liaison with the CPE, helping us with a theme and finding us a speaker from the CPE to open the Conference with a plenary session.

Obviously, we have a central location for the conference, the EKU library, and a steering committee that starts with the three of us. Monthly meetings we block out rooms and figure out how much food and beverage to order. The committee also solicits sponsorships (this year, for instance, we had four). For Kentucky Pedagogicon II (KPII), New Forums Press served as our headline sponsor, and its publisher, Doug Dollar, was our special guest. With Doug, the three of us presented a Conference session on writing a book proposal.

So far we feel successful. In each of the past two years, the Pedagogicon has drawn over two hundred conferees, a mixture of mostly faculty and a few students. Surveys indicate a high level of satisfaction with the Conference. The low $50 conference registration fee ($25 for students), the convenience of a one-day conference in a fairly close location, and quality of the presentations rank as the major positives.

Where do we go from here? Perhaps national. Later this week, less than two weeks after KPII, we have our annual FDW retreat to start the process over. Remember those old 1930's musicals where Our Gang, Mickey Rooney, or Laurel & Hardy uttered that famous phrase, "Hey gang, let's put on a show?" We did and it worked well.

Tips for Implementation

A. While you might have neither the desire to host a conference nor the support/funding to pull it off, you might consider creating a mini-conference—perhaps a half-day—on your campus.

B. Develop a theme for your conference.

C. Bring together interested colleagues from across campus to help with arrangements.

D. Secure funding for the conference from on or off-campus sources.

Discussion Questions

A. Do you believe conferences truly promote scholarship? Do they stimulate minds or encourage better teaching?

B. Would a mini-conference on pedagogy be well-received on your campus?

C. Would a mini-conference on your campus be worth the cost?

Activities

A. Brainstorm with selected colleagues ideas for a campus conference.

B. Inquire about funding for a one-day on-campus conference.

2. Making of Pedagogicon Conference Via Nifty-Nine Strategies

(Posted 12 August 2014)

http://newforums.com/making-pedagogicon-conference/

What are the best practices for integrating creativity into the classroom? Or for teaching creativity? These were some of the questions we asked at Eastern Kentucky University. We had published several books on applied created thinking, but we wanted to increase the conversations about the scholarship of teaching on our campus and in the Commonwealth. This is how we came to organize the annual Peagogicon Conference for Practicing Scholarly and Creative Teaching—an event geared for educators seeking to discover the most effective teaching practices.

The Importance of Using the Nifty-Nine Strategies

We developed the idea of the Pedagogicon by employing core applied creative thinking concepts we refer to as the nifty-nine strategies. These nine steps include: collaborating, perception shifting, piggybacking, brainstorming, glimmer-catching, playing, recognizing patterns, using metaphor, and flowing. By connecting the event's planning process back to the above strategies, we were able to create a conference that shed light on some of the most pressing issues in teaching and learning in today's higher education.

A Process for Using the Nifty-Nne Strategies for Creating A Conference

In coming up with the Pedagogicon, the three of us first **caught a glimmer** of a possibility by **collaborating** to create a 21st-century academic conference to support faculty development. For the past few years, our state organization in charge of coordinating higher education institutions in Kentucky, the Council on Postsecondary Education, sponsored a conference that combined instructional technology (IT) and faculty development. Focusing on creative approaches, we wanted to separate the strands into two distinct, but complementary conferences while focusing on the pedagogical development of faculty and administrators throughout the state.

We first needed a catchy name that combined the fundamental and powerful concepts (FPCs) of our last few books in both our Applied Creative Thinking and our It Works for Me series. After a lot of **brainstorming**, we came up with the Kentucky Pedagogicon by **recognizing and applying a pattern** in pop culture conventions, especially the growing popularity of comic book conferences—i.e., comiconcs. For our central theme, we played with the FPCs of our previous books to fashion "Practicing Scholarly and Creative Teaching."

Findings from the Pedagogicon Conference

While the Pedagogicon at EKU highlighted creative and scholarly teaching, we realized the need to integrate more student voices into the statewide conversation. As is the case with highly effective teaching, we need to seek ways to engage the student perspective. In the Noel Studio, where we held the first Pedagogicon, we commonly see students working side by side with one another as well as their instructors, thinking and learning creatively. If we pay attention to the **pattern** of collaboration and invention practices of our students, we might learn a little more about inspiring creativity in our classroom spaces.

Tips for Implementation

A. If you are unfamiliar with creative thinking strategies, read our *Introduction to Applied Creative Thinking* (New Forums, 2012).

B. Check your area/state to see if there is a void/need for such a conference.

Discussion Questions

A. Do you regard creative thinking on a par with what Derek Bok (*Our Underachieving Colleges*) calls the central skills set taught in college, critical thinking?

B. The nifty-nine creative thinking strategies were never meant to be exhaustive. Can you think of any other creative thinking strategies?

Activities

A. Choose one of the nifty-nine strategies and practice it.

B. Make a list of the pedagogical conferences held the closest to your institution. Are they sufficiently far away so that creating your own such conference could save the cost of sending colleagues away from campus?

3. Scholarship Lite

(to be published)

A few years ago, a friend of ours in the University's College of Education submitted materials to his departmental Promotion, Tenure, and Evaluation Committee, but because the bulk of his scholarship consisted of a continuing blog he wrote on K-12 education problems, the Committee found it difficult to evaluate his scholarship, for it didn't fit conveniently into the established categories. Likewise, when we joined the technological revolution with these posts to "Welcome Scholars," the question came up of how they would be evaluated as scholarship.

In our way of thinking, the profession needed additional terminology.

When *Scholarship Reconsidered: Priorities of the Professorate* (1990) appeared because "a new vision of scholarship is required" (p. 13), Ernest Boyer's typology divided scholarship into four categories:

- The **Scholarship of Discovery**: pure research
- The **Scholarship of Integration**: "making connections across the disciplines"
- The **Scholarship of Application**: "the application of knowledge"
- The **Scholarship of Teaching** (pp. 16-25).

Obviously, to evaluate these types of scholarship, various disciplines constructed rubrics that allowed for idiosyncrasies in their field. For instance, in our original discipline, English, quite prominent is the **scholarly note**, which is basically a 1200-2000-word article that focuses on a small element in a work (e.g., the grail myth in Cheever's "The Swimmer") with less research than found in a 5000-word article—i.e., scholarship short.

However, because Boyer had not offered much guidance or insight into the category, the Scholarship of Teaching evolved into the Scholarship of Teaching and Learning (SOTL). In fact, Maryellen Weimer stipulates that is the reason she wrote *Enhancing Scholarly Works on Teaching & Learning* (2006): "Virtually everyone agrees that, despite its significant contribution, Boyer's monograph, *Scholarship Reconsidered* (1990), did not clearly and precisely define what is meant by the scholarship of teaching" (p. xviii). To fill this academic gap and to "make pedagogical scholarship more credible" (p. 6), Weimer first defines SOTL as "published work on teaching and learning authored by college faculty in fields other than education" (p. 19). Then, she elucidates on SOTL as "published practitioner pedagogical work [that] can be separated into two major categories: wisdom-of-practice scholarship and research scholarship" (40).

Blogging is a category having much in common with SOTL. Some posts are basically personal narratives (to use Weimer's language) that rely more on opinions and experiences than research. Other posts are more research-oriented, what Weimer describes as "more often an isolated inquiry than part of an organized research program" that "does not generally build on previous or related work in systematic ways" (p. 42); most such scholarship does not involve a thorough knowledge of educational research practices.

For instance, for New Forums we have basically published a series of books whose general category "It Works For Me" suggests they are not weighty research tomes, but compendiums of teaching, scholarship, and creative thinking tips that have been utilized and found effective by a scholar or instructor in the field. Interestingly, the entries in the seven books in our series reflect both of Weimer's SOTL poles.

Scholarship Lite as found in blogging often resembles Weimer's "research-oriented" pole. Obviously, though, not all blogging is scholarship lite; some blogs focus on personal experience followed by recommendations/guidelines based on that experience. To us, scholarship lite necessitates a scholarly component—i.e., at least a single cited source central to the post's argument. In this sense, scholarship lite resembles a scholarly note: it is characterized by less research and exists more as an isolated inquiry than a concentrated research project.

Let's evaluate this post against those traits, and see if it comes out as scholarship lite.

- Uses some research. This post cites the threshold research of Ernest Boyer, a book by Maryellen Weimer, and even some of our publications.

- <u>Creates an argument</u>. This post tries to construct a crucial term, scholarship lite, to fill a critical void.
- <u>Doesn't claim to be educational research/concentrated project</u>. This post merely tries to establish a new concept in the scholarly vocabulary.

We need to emphasize a key idea. Scholarship lite, despite its contemporary and popular spelling, is not a pejorative term, but rather primarily descriptive. In this sense, scholarship lite is like the concept of popular literature/pop lit in simply explaining a concept; it is up to each discipline, department, and individual to decide upon its value.

One final point is worth noting. In our *It Works For Me as a Scholar-Teacher* (New Forums, 2008), we spend a chapter on "The Staircase Approach to Becoming a Published Scholar," emphasizing four consecutive steps a scholar can use to get to the top floor, publication:

1. Begin locally.
2. Present at state or regional conferences.
3. Go to national conventions with your paper.
4. Write short notes before long articles (pp. 35-37).

What we are suggesting now is an alternative approach to publication that perhaps is actually an elevator. The aspiring scholar might begin by writing blog posts that tend toward the scholarship lite pole. Posters find they often receive immediate feedback, which in turn accelerates the elevator. In addition, scholar-teachers can demonstrate the scholarship lite approach to their students, who probably feel more comfortable in the electronic arena. Win. Win.

Should we go a step further and label each post in a blog as a scholarly post or a personal post? That could be the subject of another post.

Tips for Implementation

A. Develop a couple of favored ideas you would like to share with colleagues.
B. Write up the ideas using a minimum of scholarship and distribute to friends/post on your blog.
C. Invite feedback/response to your post(s).

Discussion Questions

A. Do you find value in scholarship that contains minimal formal research?
B. Do you think blogging can be considered scholarship on any level?
C. Do you think Weimer rendered a service with her definition of SOTL?
D. Could blogging over time develop several levels depending upon the amount of scholarship/research included?

Activities

A. Survey your faculty to assess their views on SOTL and blogging.
B. Encourage colleagues to create a piece of scholarship lite.

4. Under Construction: Developing a Style Sheet for the *Journal of Faculty Development*

(Posted 25 May 2016)

http://newforums.com/developing-a-style-sheet-for-the-journal-of-faculty-development/

The past few weeks we have been reading and rereading manuscripts for a special issue of the *Journal of Faculty Development* (JFD) on the future of faculty development. Rusty has taken over as the new editor of the *Journal*, and one of the things he would like to institute is a guide on writing, writing styles, and, specifically, some major grammatical suggestions. If you were to visit New Forums' section of this website devoted to the JFD's "Author Guidelines," you would find instructions about following the APA Publication Manual (6th Edition), dealing with copyrighted materials, and the review process, but as of yet lower level concerns about grammar have not been addressed.

As a result, one of our projects has been developing these guidelines, and like our title indicates, these guidelines are "Under Construction." What follows are a rationale and some guidelines. You might remember we began addressing this issue last year with our JFD article called "The Pancake Professor and the Decline of Scholarly Writing" [29.3 (2015): 69-70].

When you have finished this post and if you have any suggestions, please email them to us at charlie.sweet@eku.edu.

Rationale

Last April Manchester *Guardian* data editor Mona Chalabi (*HT Daily Wire*) opined that grammatical correctness is actually a type of white privilege, claiming that "Grammar snobs are patronizing, pretentious, and just plain wrong." She continued, "All too often, it's a way to silence people and that's particularly offensive when it's someone who might already be struggling to speak up" (we won't point out her lack of a comma between two main clauses joined by a coordinating conjunction). In rebuttal, *Newsbuster*'s Melissa Mullins argued that grammatical correctness is more "a sign of an educated person" (http://newsbusters.org/blogs/nb/melissa-mullins/2016/04/23/angry-brit-correcting-grammar-is-racist-classist-and-sexist.

As writers of over 25 published books and 1200 articles as well as editors, we offer a third position. **Grammar exists for one purpose, clarity**, and the basic commandment of all grammar rules is "Thou shalt not confuse thy reader." Note that by our employing pronouns not in current usage, we might have violated the key rule (especially for younger readers)—and confused you. Clarity is what allows both someone "struggling to speak up" and "educated persons" to communicate on the highest level. Grammar is not a privilege, but the appropriate tool for exchanging ideas.As Barry Wylant argues, "Indeed, even language forms a type of conceptual space where the rules of spelling and grammar allow one to make sense of individual letters and words" ["Design Thinking and the Experience of Innovation," *Massachusetts Institute of Technology Design Issues* 24.2 (2008): 9].

To help our readers "make sense" of what our writers are trying to express, we ask those writers to follow the following guidelines.

Some Guidelines:

1) Use consistent formatting of author bios, including degree. For example:

Charlie Sweet, Ph.D., is the Co-Director of the Teaching & Learning Center at Eastern Kentucky University. With Hal Blythe, he has collaborated on over 1100 published works, including 23 books, literary criticism, educational research, and novels (as Quinn MacHollister).

Hal Blythe, Ph.D., is the Co-Director of the Teaching & Learning Center. With Charlie Sweet, he has collaborated on over 1100 published works, including 23 books (eight in New Forums' popular *It Works For Me* series), literary criticism, educational research, and a stint as ghostwriter of the lead novella for the *Mike Shayne Mystery Magazine*.

2) Try to avoid "There is . . .," "There are . . . ," and "It is . . . " constructions.

3) "This" and "That" are always followed by a noun.

4) Authors should use the serial comma (i.e., one comma less than the total number of items in the list) for words, phrases, or lists in a series. For example: *The journal publishes research, scholarship, and creative works.* Semi-colons appear in a list only if the individual units contain commas.

5. A comma is used to separate two main clauses joined by one of the seven coordinating conjunctions: for, and, but, or, nor, so (that), yet. Place the comma before the conjunction.

6. Avoid "when" and "where" after "is" in definitions.

7. Don't use redundancies such as "the reason why" or "is because."

8. Do not substitute "would be" for the present or past verb tense.

9. Use pronouns properly (e.g., "Terry was the kind of student that took tests poorly" should be "Terry was the kind of student who took tests poorly."

10. Hyphenate two consecutive modifiers being used as a singular adjective (e.g., I developed a six-minute video on degree-completion students).

11. Use introductory commas (e.g., Therefore, I conclude that flipping goes well).

12. If APA does not provide a format for a reference, make one up as best you can following close examples. Be consistent if you have to make up similar references.

Any suggestions?

Tips for Implementation

A. Since clarity is the goal of effective writing, work to make all your correspondence from your program—with or without GrammarCheck—grammatically correct.

B. Carefully proofread pieces you submit to publication. Always read a piece twice—once for its sense and again for its grammar. And it never hurts to have a colleague look it over (with three sets of eyes on everything we write, we still miss things).

C. Offer to mentor colleagues in manuscript publication.

Discussion Questions

A. Do you think proper grammar is important in manuscripts?

B. Do you read your students' papers for grammar, or do you consider that something only English teachers have to worry about?

C. Do you agree that proper grammar is a form of academic snobbery?

D. Do you agree that clarity is the most important function of proper grammar?

E. Do you think a perfectly written piece from a grammatical standpoint is ever accepted for publication despite deficiencies in its content?

Activities

A. Volunteer to edit a colleague's manuscript, including line editing for grammar.

B. Establish a PLC on manuscript preparation.

5. Collaboration and the Scholar

(to be published)

The current issue of the *Chronicle of Higher Education* (November 14, 2014) carries an essay that provides a rationale for the traditional role of the solitary scholar. In "Leave Me Alone," Magdalena Kay laments the current trend toward collaborative writing in academia, arguing, "I believe the best work, particularly that dinosaur known as the single-author scholarly book or article, often gets done in solitude" (B20).

We beg to differ. Each of us began with single-authored pieces, but over the years we have come to recognize that collaboration has made us better writers. While our chief constellation involves a triad, we wrote *Teaching Applied Creative Thinking* (2013) as a quartet, and Hal and Charlie recently co-wrote *Achieving Excellence in Teaching* (2014) with two different members singing in their quartet (hey, even the Beatles changed drummers). Rusty has likewise written with others, and recently the three of us partnered with two graduate students on an article about flipping the classroom.

Kay is right that while collaboration is becoming the norm in the hard and social sciences, the humanities still favor single authorship. The three of us came out of the traditional departments of English, but now like Whitman's spider we constantly cast out filaments trying to connect with other writers. Why? For the long answer, check out *It Works For Me, Collaboratively* (2006), *It Works For Me as a Scholar-Teacher* (2008), *It Works For Me: Becoming a Publishing Scholar/Researcher* (2010), or our chapter on "Collaborating" in *Introduction to Applied Creative Thinking* (2012). Here, we'll just suggest some short answers.

More ideas. In the old days we relied on our students, actual works of literature, and critical works to stimulate our brain cells. Now that we have transitioned into predominantly administrative roles, we find our colleagues aid us directly or indirectly in producing scholarship. Obvious, as the genesis of this piece proves, we still read the literature in the field, but we depend more on bouncing our ideas of each other. If two heads are better than one in brainstorming, what are three, four? We've seen the research on ideation levels improving from a single source to multiple sources an incredible 600%.

Better ideas. A major problem in single authorship is critical thinking. Book writers often have a pool of peers or an editor to guide them through the process. We learned more about writing from our former editor at *Writer's Digest* than we did in graduate school. Other voices provide perspective, making us shift our commas and concepts.

Stimuli to persist. When one writes alone, it is too easy to succumb to distractions—checking the email, raiding the fridge, going for a walk—but the social-ability of writing with others means you're stuck for the entire time period you've chosen to work on the task. And it's more fun. Someone else can crack a joke, tell an anecdote, or provide that charge you need to continue when your mind is telling you a thousand other places you could be. Moreover, collaborators often provide that simple, enthusiastic "Hey, good idea" or "Atta-girl" that keeps you going better than Red Bull.

Compensate for your weaknesses. Charlie and Hal are not as technologically competent as Rusty. Rusty and Hal don't follow pop culture as much as Charlie. Charlie and Rusty don't understand absolute phrases and appositives as well as Hal (to this day Charlie never uses "lie" or "lay" without first consulting Hal). Charlie comes up with ideas well, Rusty synthesizes them better, and Hal organizes the thoughts best. And sometimes it takes all three of us to figure out the proper APA citation.

In the beginning we all write alone. The three of us wouldn't have discovered the advantages and joy of collabo-writing had we not tried it. Is it for every scholar? Probably not, but you won't know if you don't give it a go.

Tips For Implementation

A. Consider a project on which you might collaborate with a colleague or colleagues.

B. Identify those colleagues who might be most open to collaboration and valuable as collaborators.

C. Contact prospective collaborators and discuss potential projects.

Discussion Questions

A. Do you work better alone or in collaboration?
B. Have you ever attempted a collaborative project?
C. What do you consider the pros and cons of collaboration?

Activities

A. Attempt a collaborative presentation, publication, or even a jointly-taught class.
B. Organize a roundtable discussion on the strengths and weaknesses of collaboration.

ASSESSMENT

By Charlie Sweet, Hal Blythe & Russell Carpenter

1. Going to WAR: Using a Weekly Activities Report for Assessment, Part I

(Posted 9 March 2016)

http://newforums.com/going-to-war-using-a-weekly-activities-report-for-assessment/

Want a simple assessment tool for your CTL, one that tracks your daily activities while providing you with a detailed read-out of what activities dominate your unit? A few years ago our dean expressed both an educational and oversight interest in learning what our CTL—here it's the Teaching & Learning Center--actually does—i.e., how can she justify continuing to support funding our unit? At first, we thought of our response as merely making our boss happy—what we've already discussed as the number one job of a CTL—but then we realized such a response had terrific P.R. value and it could serve as an effective assessment tool.

To create a weekly report, we used our CTL's strategic plan as a template. The process was relatively painless since when we established our strategic plan, we followed our university's format. First, list your goals:

1. GOAL 1: Effectively administer the unit (list here the over-arching university goals that this goal addresses).
2. GOAL 2: Provide venue/facilitation for the University (university goals).
3. GOAL 3: Provide high-quality professional development (university goals).

Next, the University asked us to run its Bachelor of Individualized Studies (BIS) Program, so we added one:

4. GOAL 4: Effectively administer the BIS Program (university goals).

Along the way, we also found we were being asked to perform various tasks that did not conform to our four goals, so a new category was tacked on:

5. Miscellaneous.

Under each of these goals, we created a list of objectives. For instance, Goal 3 of professional development has ten items:

- Objective 1: The TLC will provide faculty and staff with cutting-edge pedagogy information/training.
- Objective 2: The TLC will provide faculty and staff with scholarship training.
- Objective 3: The TLC will coordinate orientations for such groups as New Faculty, Part-Time New Faculty, First-Year Course Faculty, and Teaching Assistants.
- Objective 4: The TLC will administer the Faculty Consultation Program (FCP).
- Objective 5: The TLC will sponsor and coordinate several types of Professional Learning Communities (PLCS) (e.g., traditional PLCs, Breakfast and a Books, and Creative Communities).
- Objective 6: The TLC will facilitate, when needed, specialized faculty and staff professional development workshops (e.g., our Teaching & Learning Innovations Series).

- Objective 7: The TLC will administer the Faculty Innovators (FI) program.
- Objective 8: The TLC will liaise with the Council on Postsecondary Education's (CPE) Faculty Development Workgroup.
- Objective 9: The TLC will collaborate with the Noel Studio.

Interestingly, these objectives have morphed over the past ten years with some objectives added, deleted, or synthesized. For instance, as we were writing this post, we noticed that over the years Objective 3 on orientations has expanded from its original single charge, New Faculty Orientation (NFO). When we began the Center, we were put on a committee of faculty charged with running NFO. Gradually, we came to realize that most of that group really didn't want to be doing it, had no background in professional development, and were just overseeing a program that had been passed on down to them. Slowly, we suggested some changes that reduced the orientation's length from five days to three and cut costs in half. Our most important change, however, was redirecting NFO's focus to the importance of each professor's major duty, teaching. When NFO became an efficient, cost-saving process, others around the University noticed. Part-time Orientation was added to our plates. Then the Dean of the Graduate School asked us to facilitate a session for his Teaching Assistants. Later, First-Year-Programs asked us to present their program, and recently the Student Success unit inquired if we can help them.

Success begets success, sometimes so much that we can't handle all the requests.

Objectives come and go. Six years ago, for instance, the University asked us to address Senate Bill 1 that created a seamless transition between secondary and higher education. Thus, we created CARTE (though we can no longer remember for what the acronym stood). Also, the provost has had several temporary initiatives we've been tasked with helping. And we've developed a few programs, such as Scholarship Week and the Pedagogicon, that have grown to major importance.

Next time we'll explain how we use the WAR for assessment and provide some particulars.

2. Going to WAR: Using a Weekly Activities Report for Assessment, Part II

(Posted 16 March 2016)

http://newforums.com/going-to-war-using-a-weekly-assessment-report-for-assessment-part-ii/

As we explained in our previous post, the Weekly Assessment Report—the WAR—provides an excellent methodology for assessment. Unlike annual reports, the WAR provides a weekly snapshot of the activities that dominate our CTL's schedule as well as an easy way to check on items that are registering less frequently. As a result, we can respond to challenges and opportunities immediately rather than being months late.

Here's how the WAR works. Each Friday morning we type up a report by starting with the basic shell of our strategic plan. For instance, under Goal 3, Objective 1 states, "The TLC [The Teaching & Learning Center] will provide faculty and staff with cutting-edge pedagogy information/training." The objective specifies a couple of aims. One, we are not going to go back and rehearse materials that have become commonplace. The faculty handbook places responsibility on individual faculty for staying current; our job is to help there, while faculty will have to learn the foundational material (e.g., what are Boyer's four areas of scholarship) on their own. Secondly, the inclusion of the "staff" suggests why we often use the more inclusive term "professional" (e.g., Profession Learning Community). No, we do not use staff because we offer pure staff training in such things as proper use of chemicals, but because at our university the administrative staff (e.g., the provost, deans, academic vice-presidents, director of Public Relations) actually teach everything from first-year to graduate courses.

At one time we were fulfilling Goal 3, Objective I through a series of what we called roundtables. When we were asked by our then dean to offer not only pedagogical training but in the fall to offer the roundtables as a way of various groups, especially those in our college (University Programs), to be able to present to the faculty at large what services they render, we envisioned these roundtables as active-learning workshops. Thus, back then, our WAR would mention talks by the University Co-op Education area, Study Abroad, University Counselling, and the Disabilities Office interspersed with workshops on flipping the classroom and SOTL. What we came to realize was that by spreading out the presenters' areas, we had lost a sharp focus on our main mission (Helping Teachers Help Students Learn Deeply).

Therefore, this semester we inaugurated the Teaching and Learning Innovation Series (TLI) to refocus on the objective's "cutting-edge" pedagogy. Instead of 20 presentations that ricocheted between service and pedagogy, we emphasized such obviously teaching concerns as critical reading, metacognition, intuitive teaching, quality matters, and designing visual syllabi. We also cut the number in half, figuring that offering half the number might increase attendance.

We made other subtle changes after looking through last semester's WARs. We noticed that we had set up workshops on all five days, so any faculty member looking for continuity would be unable to find it. Therefore, this year we scheduled every event on Thursday afternoon. The registrar informed us that Friday classes were being scheduled less and less, and the most open times (i.e., fewest classes) were 8:00 a.m. and 3:30 p.m., so we chose 3:00-4:00. And to give us a better sense of who was attending, when we put out announcements of our events, we listed a registration URL. Furthermore, we created a logo for the TLI series, and after each event we emailed its participants a simple electronic evaluation. Finally, we created flyers, electronic and paper, for each presentation, handing out the flyer for event 4 at event 3 and including the flyers as attachments when we used the campus email system to advertise our series. Rusty, our master tweeter, took to Twitter to advertise and provide real-time updates of our programming.

Already this semester, attendance at our sessions has increased. Our workshop on metacognitive strategies, for instance, received over 50 registrants, so we had to move it twice to larger rooms that could accommodate such a crowd. In fact, that workshop proved so successful that we added a second session on metacognitive strategies for later in the semester. Another improvement has been an increase in email traffic. This morning, for example, we found an email from a metacognition participant with a source he "hoped" we mentioned at our next session.

And all this change came about in just one goal's one objective. From the beginning we've said that so much of what we do at our CTL is in its beta stage. The WAR has provided us with an instrument to make informed changes on the fly.

Tips For Implementation (Parts I and II)

A. Determine the goals for your faculty development program.
B. Determine the steps you will take to achieve these goals.
C. Construct a document that will allow you to record your implementation of those steps and their success.

Discussion Questions

A. Do you have a formal statement of goals for your faculty development program?
B. How do your goal line up with your institution's goals/strategic plan?
C. How willing and/or able are you to adjust your goals and steps toward them?

Activities

A. Create a document listing your program's goal and potential steps to achieve them—i.e., an action plan.
B. Assess your success in carrying out your plan.

3. An Innovative Plan for Assessing Faculty Development

(Posted 4 May 2016)

http://newforums.com/an-innovative-plan-for-assessing-faculty-development/

Sunday night we had supper with assessment guru Peggy Maki, author of the forthcoming *Real-Time Assessment*, and while she was picking apart her eggplant parmigiana, we were picking her brain on how to assess faculty development. While we didn't learn anything startling, we received sufficient help so that next year we can try a new form of professional development assessment. One caveat. Traditionally, assessment types focus on student learning, so we have had to translate Peggy's thoughts into faculty learning.

A Very Short History of Assessing Faculty Development

When we started in faculty development at the beginning of this century, the go-to form of assessment was quantitative analysis. Administrators asked for the number of seats filled in each event and how many faculty were reached during the year (typically 10%). The next phase was the Satisfaction Survey. Along with books and take-aways/hand-outs, faculty were given a short assessment tool with a Likert scale and asked to rate their satisfaction with the event from 1-5. From satisfaction we moved to learning surveys. Same idea, same scale, but with questions such as:
- Did you learn anything valuable at today's workshop?
- Do you plan to implement anything you learned today?

The major problem was our lack of follow-up. Regrettably, a year or two later, we never asked the workshop's original participants if anything they learned helped their students learn.

Now as postsecondary education is being required by the public, accrediting agencies, and even state governments to demonstrate student learning, so too professional developers are asked to show that faculty participants learned something, they did something, and greater student learning resulted.

The problem has always been: how do we find evidence that links faculty learning from Centers for Teaching and Learning (CTLs) directly to student learning? Thanks to Peggy we have some ideas.

Some Guidelines

Sunday night Peggy introduced us to another belief of current assessment experts—quick feedback. While providing that feedback is most important for students, especially those in danger of flunking a course/flunking out of school, faculty likewise need some sort of systematic appraisal of their teaching immediately. In short, real-time assessment has become a necessity—the sooner the message is delivered, the faster the professor can aid students.

1. Obviously, a professional development assessment needs to be <u>immediate</u>. Faculty must get some fast feedback. Early and timely interventions can head off problems later, reinforce good ideas, and point out problems with approaches being used.

2. Create a <u>manageable cohort</u>. Try to find a group that can be tracked without a lot of hard work and that has some reason to be thought of together. Having early and constant access to the group helps.

3. <u>Focus on one thing</u> or just a few things to assess. Make it/them fundamental and powerful concepts. Too many assessments try to accomplish too much. Start small.

4. Faculty like student learners need <u>frequent iteration</u> of the fundamental and powerful concept(s). If at all possible try to theme a semester or even a year.

5. <u>Emphasize the application of the idea</u> over simply knowing the idea. Figure out a way to evaluate the concept applied/in action.

6. In dealing with a cohort, try to develop a <u>common language</u>. Use the same words in various opportunities.

A Tentative Plan

Well, as Alice says in Wonderland, "It seems very pretty," but how do we translate these guidelines into a workable plan? If there is such a thing as real-time assessment, then there's also real-time planning, which is how you are receiving this material—in real time as we sort through the ideas. Admittedly, our plans aren't fleshed out, but here's what we'd like to do in the next academic year.

1. <u>Immediacy</u>. We'd like to implement a faculty development program next fall that would give our cohort feedback during the same time frame.

2. <u>Manageable Cohort</u>. Our hope is to use the new faculty that will be joining us in the fall. They are manageable in that the cohort is usually less than fifty, they have a commonality in their newness, and as purveyors of New Faculty Orientation, we usually see them first and collect an email list of them before they even arrive on campus.

3. <u>One-Thing Focus</u>. As we have just written a book for New Forums called *Transforming Your Students into Deep Learners* (2016) and provide eight excellent strategies for so doing, a theme of deep learning would be in our wheelhouse. Besides, in her presentation to the faculty, Peggy discussed deep learning, especially in the sense of being able to transfer knowledge, as the goal of higher education.

4. <u>Frequent Iteration</u>. Since we helm the Teaching & Learning Innovations Series of workshops and most series consist of ten events, each workshop could focus on one deep learning strategy. And we have eight strategies to form the basis for eight workshops.

5. <u>Emphasize Application</u>. Whatever we present, we would have to persuade our cohort to apply during the fall. How do we assess the student learning resulting from that application? As we said, this plan is a work in progress, and here is the stickiest point, but luckily we are running a professional learning community (PLC) this semester on the latest on peer observation.

6. <u>Common Language</u>. This guideline is easy to fulfill. We can hand out our book during New Faculty Orientation and even go over the basic concepts and definitions before the semester starts. *Transforming Your Students into Deep Learners* can function simultaneously as our dictionary and sourcebook. Maybe we should run the entire cohort of new faculty like a PLC.

Conclusion

We have a basic plan, four months, an able body of instructors—ten Faculty Innovators (FIs) to help us—and a retreat with the FIs next month. Don't you just love it when a good plan starts to come together?

Tips For Implementation

A. Consider exactly what you wish to achieve with your faculty development program and consider developing a theme to connect various events.

B. Determine the simplest assessment tool you can fashion, allowing both you and faculty members to see the strengths and weaknesses of the program.

C. Prepare for long-term follow-up to the immediate assessment.

Discussion Questions

A. Do you currently have an assessment protocol for your program?

B. How successful has your assessment been?

C. Have you considered attention to the long-time results of your program?

Activities

A. Fashion an assessment tool that will call on faculty members to apply what they learn from the program, and evaluate results.

B. Solicit ideas from faculty on what strategies might enhance your program.

AFTERWORD

Simplify. Synthesize. Strategize. Implement. Assess.

At the end of most academic meetings, the facilitator usually gives out the marching orders—i.e., what are the next steps. After writing this book, we're issuing some guidelines about what you can do with the fifty-plus essays you have read.

3SIA (Simplify, Synthesize, Strategize, Implement, and Assess) offers a basic summary of the next steps.

1. Establish regular meetings with your boss as well as those with whom you work. Ascertain exactly what your boss wants from you both now and in the future.

2. Develop a newsletter or report format (e.g., WAR) that allows you to keep both your boss and those with whom you work aware of what's going on.

3. Regularly revisit your strategic plan. Make certain that all your activities fall within the scope of that plan.

4. Establish credibility and a rapport with your institution's faculty through surveys, advisory boards, prompt email response, a currency with hot trends and a program such as Faculty Innovators.

5. Never be satisfied with what you are accomplishing. Utilize some of the creative and design thinking strategies we've suggested.

6. Do what must be done to become interwoven into the fabric of your institution by aligning with the school's strategic plan and by building faculty and administrative relationships.

7. Just as an instructor shoots for 100% class participation, try to reach as many faculty as you can.

8. Build a solid library—both virtual and on-ground—that can be used by faculty and you.

9. Serve as a conduit to bring together individuals and groups from across campus for collaborations.

10. Cultivate productive relationships with your counterparts at schools in your state and region. Consider forming a faculty development network.

11. Attend conferences and participate in webinars both to gain information and to make contacts with colleagues in the field.

12. Be willing to take risks in order to make significant advances.

13. Know your limits in terms of resources, personnel, funding, and time/space, and avoid the pitfall of trying to be all things to all people.

ABOUT THE AUTHORS

Charlie Sweet, Ph.D. (Florida State University, 1970), is the Co-Director of the Teaching & Learning Center at Eastern Kentucky University. With Hal, he has collaborated on over 1100 published works, including 23 books, literary criticism, educational research, and novels (as Quinn MacHollister).

Hal Blythe, Ph.D. (University of Louisville, 1972), is the Co-Director of the Teaching & Learning Center. With Charlie, he has collaborated on over 1100 published works, including 23 books (eight in New Forums' popular It Works For Me series), literary criticism, educational research, and a stint as ghostwriter of the lead novella for the *Mike Shayne Mystery Magazine*.

Russell Carpenter, Ph.D. (University of Central Florida, 2009), is Executive Director of the Noel Studio for Academic Creativity and Program Director of Applied Creative Thinking at Eastern Kentucky University where he is also Associate Professor of English. Dr. Carpenter has published on the topic of creative thinking, among other areas, including three texts by New Forums Press: *Introduction to Applied Creative Thinking* (with Charlie Sweet and Hal Blythe, 2012), *Teaching Applied Creative Thinking* (with Charlie Sweet, Hal Blythe, and Shawn Apostel, 2013), and *It Works for Me, Flipping the Classroom: Shared Tips for Effective Teaching*, (with Hal Blythe and Charlie Sweet, 2015). He has guest edited or co-edited special issues of the *Journal of Faculty Development* on social media and the future of faculty development. In addition, he has taught courses in creative thinking in EKU's Minor in Applied Creative Thinking, which was featured in the *New York Times* in February 2014, and rhetoric and composition in the Department of English.

www.ingramcontent.com/pod-product-compliance
Lightning Source LLC
Chambersburg PA
CBHW081148230426
43664CB00018B/2844